HOW TO BECOME TRULY WEALTHY

MONEY IS THE MEANS NOT THE GOAL

SIRSHREE

Money is the Means, Not the Goal
By **Sirshree** Tejparkhi

Copyright © Tejgyan Global Foundation
All Rights Reserved 2020

Tejgyan Global Foundation is a charitable organization
with its headquarters in Pune, India.

ISBN : 978-81-8415-724-6

Published by WOW Publishings Pvt. Ltd., India

First edition published in December 2020

Printed and bound by Trinity Academy, Pune, INDIA

Copyrights are reserved with Tejgyan Global Foundation and publishing rights are vested exclusively with WOW Publishings Pvt. Ltd. This book is sold subject to the condition that it shall not by way of trade or otherwise, be lent, resold, hired out, or otherwise circulated without the publisher's prior written consent in any form of binding or cover other than that in which it is published and without a similar condition including this condition being imposed on the subsequent purchaser and without limiting the rights under copyright reserved above, no part of this publication may be reproduced, stored in or introduced into a retrieval system, or transmitted, in any form, or by any means, electronic, mechanical, photocopying, recording or otherwise, without the prior written permission of both the copyright owner and the above-mentioned publisher of this book. Any person who does any unauthorized act in relation to this publication may be liable to criminal prosecution and civil claims for damages.

Although the author and publisher have made every effort to ensure accuracy of content in this book, they hereby disclaim any liability to any party for any loss, damage, or disruption caused by errors or omissions, resulting from negligence, accident, or any other cause. Readers are advised to take full responsibility to exercise discretion in understanding and applying the content of this book.

*To those
who realize the value of material prosperity
as a powerful means to attain the real purpose of life—
the purpose of awakening to the true Self, abiding in it,
and being instrumental for awakening others.*

Contents

	Preface	7
1.	More Money or More Understanding?	11
2.	Channelize Money and Become Rich	17
3.	Language and Definition of Money	23
4.	Three Delusions About Money	26
5.	Thirteen Money Myths	30
6.	Let Money Flow	37
7.	Be the Owner of Money, Not its Caretaker	41
8.	Do Not Block Money	44
9.	Set the Right Aim for Earning Money	48
10.	Focus on What is Gained, Not on What is Spent	51
11.	Use Money for Needs, Not for Wants	54
12.	Lack of Money or Right Thinking?	58
13.	Learning How to Learn	63
14.	The Money Mantra	68

15.	Let Money Beget More Money	71
16.	Don't Envy the Rich	74
17.	Use Money to Boost Health and Happiness	76
18.	Stop the Meaningless Rat-race for Money	79
19.	Consciously Sow the Seeds of Faith	83
20.	Time is Also Money	93
21.	The Law of Nature	96
22.	Attain Real Wealth	100
23.	Neither be a Worldly Person, Nor a Recluse	103
24.	Contemplation	108

Preface

*With the right understanding,
money is a boon; else it is a bane.
Life is a joy when money is a boon.
Life is sorrow when money is a bane.*

Today, people have various beliefs about what real wealth is. Some consider money and riches as wealth, while others consider health as wealth. Some consider the availability of quality time as real wealth.

In this increasingly fast-paced world, money has become the biggest priority in almost everyone's life. It is obvious that man needs money to fulfil his needs. However, with the passage of time and changing needs, the demand for money has also changed. We find people trying to earn more and more money. Despite having fulfilled all their needs, some people continue earning money as they do not know what else they can do. They seek happiness in watching their bank balance grow, not knowing that it is an endless pursuit.

So, where has all this started from? What is the basic motive behind their endless pursuit? The basic motive is to be happy. But are they really happy?

A survey was conducted among the elderly and the terminally ill to find out what their most common regrets were. One among the top five regrets was, "I wish I had let myself be happier."

Isn't it ironical? After toiling hard throughout their lives, if people are going to have such regrets at the end of their life, the whole pursuit is rendered futile, a pursuit undertaken in the wrong direction. So, is there something wrong with their understanding of happiness itself?

If we observe the lives of the materially rich people, we can see that material riches do not guarantee happiness. In fact, there are many affluent people who are riddled with anxiety, restlessness, and dissatisfaction in their lives.

We see some people chase money, while others immerse themselves in spiritual practices and shun material riches. There is nothing wrong with acquiring money or satisfying material needs, but deriving permanent bliss and peace from them is impossible, just like extracting oil from stone is impossible.

The truth is that money is just a mode of exchange. It is one of the means towards fulfilling our goals. But we commit the mistake of making money our goal! As a physical commodity, it has a value and substance. However, with time, people have projected their insecurities, need for power and desires onto money and tried to use that as a means to secure themselves mentally. Much of the desire for power and other desires are linked to money. When money begins to drive our desires, there is no end to wanting more.

The key is to attain the state of joy and peace while being in the midst of the marketplace, satisfying our worldly needs. Instead of working for money, let the laws of life work for us, bringing us an abundance of money to fulfil all our needs.

What is your relationship with money? What does money mean to you? Is it worthwhile spending a third of your lifetime in earning money regardless of whether or not you actually spend it?

This book explains how you can set the right equation with money. It explains the wrong equation that leads to money problems and also dispels prevalent myths and limiting beliefs about money. The book expounds the simple rules of how prosperity flows in life. Replete with examples and simple exercises, it throws light on how you can create the right mindset to attract and sustain prosperity in your life.

Most of us generally overlook the simple fact that money is merely a means of exchange for smooth functioning in this world. It is a boon to make our lives simpler, but many of us complicate our lives by making money a curse.

Let us understand prosperity and learn to use money in the right way. We should use money; money should not use us. By understanding the invisible laws of life, we will not only beget money, but also attain the wealth of wisdom, love, courage, and health. One who possesses all these types of wealth is indeed truly wealthy.

With the understanding that money is a means, let us learn the secret of reinforcing this means through this book. May we achieve success on this path!

More Money or More Understanding?

*No one becomes rich by earning more money.
One becomes rich by attaining more understanding about money.
When you attain the right understanding about money,
your money problems end.*

'Earning more money solves all problems.' Is this true, or is it just a false notion?

One who earns Rs. 5,000 thinks that earning Rs. 10,000 will solve his money problems. Another person making Rs. 10,000 believes that earning Rs. 15,000 will surely get him out of all problems. The one who earns Rs. 15,000 feels that he will be free from financial worries if he starts earning Rs. 25,000. And what about the man who makes Rs. 25,000? Is he free from all worries? Even he believes that earning Rs. 40,000 will solve his financial problems. This means, it is not the money, but the 'understanding about money' that can resolve monetary issues.

Attaining the right understanding about money is very important. And it becomes even more crucial if one is pursuing the spiritual path. Else, all his time would be spent in resolving worldly matters, that would move the spiritual quest to the backburner. Observations show that many spiritual seekers, who set out on the path of making money, spent their entire life in becoming financially stable. They never returned to the pursuit of the Truth again.

This is because no amount of money seemed enough. They kept trying to accumulate more and more wealth. They never felt the satisfaction of having earned enough to start focusing on their real goal of attaining the Truth. Despite having abundant wealth, they led life with the feeling of scarcity.

Man may make a lot of money, but in his ignorance, he still feels its lack. No one becomes rich by earning more money. One becomes rich by attaining more understanding about money. The right understanding about money destroys the very root cause of all money problems. As soon as this root cause is uprooted, the lack of wealth disappears from life.

If more money means more satisfaction, then all the high-earning people would have been the happiest of all. But countless instances prove that this is not true.

'Understanding money' encompasses understanding how we should use money, understanding investment, growth, expenditure, savings, false notions about money, the importance of good money habits, etc. This understanding makes us wealthy in the real sense. That is why it is prudent to spend some money and earn the right understanding about it.

> Once upon a time, a saint gave a philosopher's stone to a poor man for a month. This stone could turn iron into gold. With the desire to make gold out of scrap iron, this man went to the market. He learned that the price of iron had grown by Rs. 20 on the same day. On inquiry, he realized that the prices might fall in a couple of days. He patiently waited for the prices to reduce but in vain. After a month, the saint returned for his precious stone. It was only then that the man realized his foolishness that no matter how much the price of iron increased,

it could never equal that of gold. It would have been profitable for him even if he had bought the iron at a higher price and turned it into gold. But he failed to understand this earlier.

We often hear people saying, "I earn so much, yet money does not stay for long. It just vanishes in no time." The fact is that the habit of spending money for wrong purposes does not allow money to stay in one's hands.

If money does not stay for long, even after earning it, then it is only because of the wrong money habits. Spending money carelessly is like making a tiny hole in the bottom of a ship. This tiny hole can sink the whole ship. These little holes are the petty expenses. Be aware of such petty expenses; the holes that have formed in your 'life' boat. Stay away from the bad habits described below. If one can break these habits, then the same money can turn into a great blessing for them.

The equation that represents the first and the last cause of money problems is:

Carelessness + Laziness + Wrong Habits − Understanding
= Money Problem

Let us understand each of the elements of this equation in detail.

Carelessness

The habit of carelessness and extravagant spending aggravates money problems.

Many a time people with such habits rely on fate. They either blow away all their money, or become misers. One should never waste time depending on fate, getting entangled with fortune tellers, or seeking wealth in lotteries.

Winning jackpots in lotteries induces the habit of spending money thoughtlessly. With the passage of time, all the money gets spent, but the hunger for fulfilling desires doesn't die down.

Winning lotteries can never solve fiscal problems. This is because such people stop acquiring skills needed for earning money. They remain incompetent. Their faith shifts from their own abilities and competencies towards ways of making easy money. They become slaves to money.

The desire of fulfilling more desires is the cause of unhappiness. After all the wealth is spent, man is still unable to fulfill his desires. Various cravings and wants keep arising and nagging him for fulfillment. Such individuals lead a glum life.

Money earned without any effort either breeds incompetence or reinforces one's hunger for desires and habits of extravagance. Hence, it is advisable to enhance the earning ability and achieve self-confidence. On the other hand, one, who relies on hard work, is always self-reliant and always remains healthy. He leads a life of contentment and peace.

One can clearly notice the difference between the lives of the first and the second type of people. Therefore, never shy away from hard work.

Laziness

Habits of laziness and procrastination obstruct the inflow of money. For example, delay in depositing funds in the bank results in loss of the interest that could have been earned. Laziness makes a person either penny-pinching or poor. Both these extremes are highly disadvantageous.

Wrong Habits

Here is a list of some of the wrong habits that one should be cautious of:

1) Borrowing or lending money without giving it a second thought.
2) Inability to say 'no' to anyone.

3) Shying away from bargaining, with notions like, 'How can I bargain here? What will people think?' Such thinking leads to the habit of spending more every time for what may cost less.

4) Giving money to anyone who asks for it, without ascertaining if that person genuinely needs it.

5) Inability to save money and indulging in unnecessary expenditure.

6) Piling up the number of creditors.

7) The habit of dwelling on ways to earn easy money (gambling, lotteries, betting, etc.).

Understanding

Financial troubles never end if there is a lack of understanding about money. We should use money, and it should not be the other way round, where money starts using us. Hence, let us respect money and not nurse feelings like jealousy or hatred towards it.

Wealth has been created for the self-expression of mankind; mankind is not created to glorify wealth. Money is a path, not the destination. Everything is abundant on this earth, including money. Hence, let's bear this understanding about money and use it appropriately.

If a person breaks out of the formula 'Carelessness + Laziness + Wrong habits − Understanding = Money problems', then his money problems will end once and for all.

Financial problems end for those who get rid of their addictions, carelessness, and laziness and enhance their understanding about money. Else, financial constraints continue to plague people throughout their life.

People do not know how to search for and dig out the treasure of prosperity. A few bad habits and lack of understanding about money stops them from stacking up this treasure. But the good news is that this treasure of prosperity can be built by imbibing just a few good practices. These practices are explained in more detail in the ensuing chapters.

In the earlier story of the poor man with the philosopher's stone, the poor man remained poor as he lacked understanding. Are we too repeating the same mistake? Our saint, the angel of death, can come at any time to take back our philosopher's stone (life). Let us use this precious stone in the right way while we have it.

Channelize Money and Become Rich

*Spending money carelessly is like
digging a small hole
at the bottom of the ship.
It can cause the ship to sink.*

There is a saying: 'Practice makes one perfect.' But there's a missing word in this adage. It should rather be, '*Perfect* practice makes one perfect.' To become rich, practice correctly on the following law of nature:

Whatever you pay attention to, grows in your life.

As you read this book and begin to pay attention to your financial development, you open yourself to the possibility of growth of true wealth in your life. Thereby, it will be easier for you to pursue your actual goal, because money will help pave the path for you.

Now that you've made a list of wrong or careless habits related to money based on the previous chapter, the next step would be to give right attention and direction to your current finances. First of all, start maintaining a monthly record of the cash inflow and outflow, how many times you have bargained for items, etc.

Money cannot be appropriately channelized unless you have an account of each and every penny. Without proper channelization, money no longer remains money, but turns into a free flying bird, which one cannot manage to keep in one's hands.

You can start by contemplating on this question, "What exactly happened to the money that I earned? Where and how was that money spent?" You can note the answers to these questions on paper or preferably in an account book (diary of expenses). This small step will give you a new perspective on your finances. You will then be able to decide where and how your money should be spent henceforth.

A person always complains about dearth of time, despite having a lot of time. This is because he does not know exactly how and where his time is being spent. Similarly, money flows in everyone's life, but most people remain largely ignorant about how and where they are spending it.

Just as the tasks that eat up most of our time are known as 'time-killers', similarly the expenses that eat up most of our money should be termed as money-killers. Beware of such money-killers. Wherever you see money-killers in your daily life, work on them immediately.

The monthly expense chart

With a bird's eye view, if a family man accounts for his monthly expenses, they can be broadly categorized under various expense heads. A sample spread is provided below:

Particulars of expenses	**% of total income**
House Rent & Taxes	20 %
Telephone & Electricity	10 %
Groceries, etc.	18 %
Fruits & Vegetables	06 %
Clothes	06 %
Children's Fees	06 %

Petrol/Transport	08 %
Medicines	03 %
Guests, Festivals, etc.	03 %
Petty Expenses	08 %
Total	**88 %**
Saving	**12%**

You can try and prepare a monthly budget in this manner. Note down where exactly your money is being spent. Then with the help of the information given in this book, you can start working on improving your finances. Otherwise, it could become difficult to identify how and where your hard-earned money is draining out.

Maintaining a balance sheet is not just a necessity for those who pay income tax or run huge businesses. Every person should be aware of each item that comes in and goes out. This will help them make quick and better decisions in times of need.

Learn to give to yourself too

People often spend their money at the grocery store, electricity bills, mobile bills, etc. They spend this money to fulfill their needs, but the most important part that one should contemplate is, **"Have I ever given money to myself?"**

Very often, we give love to others, but not to ourselves. We give time to others, but never take time out for ourselves. We pay attention to everything in the world, but fail to give attention to ourselves. This is the fundamental reason why we do not grow to the extent we can by giving ourselves the necessary money, love, time, and attention.

Now you need to decide how much percentage of money, time, love, and attention you would want to give to yourself. Here's what you can do. You can divide your income into ten equal parts. Whether your income is high or low, whatever amount you earn, split the money into ten parts. Out of these ten parts, give one part to yourself. This means that you keep one part aside for your growth and wellbeing. As you read on, you will see how you can use this portion as a seed to reap an abundant harvest after a period of time.

To avoid wealth woes in your life, making ten parts of your income and keeping aside one part works wonders. Otherwise, people squander their savings for satisfying their non-essential desires like entertainment. They organize parties, buy things, and so forth. Thus they spend all their savings. They squander the interest earned on long-term savings and find themselves back in the same situation of paucity.

People always believe that they can become rich and solve their money problems by earning more money. As we have seen in the previous chapters, people with such thinking never get rich. On the contrary, they live under a lot of pressure and always feel the pinch of paucity; because they do not know the secret of money.

The Seed of the Great Tree of Prosperity

Make a small rule for yourself: Whenever you get or earn Rs. 10,000, tell yourself that you have received Rs. 9,000 only. Out of Rs. 10,000, this Rs.1,000 will be kept aside as a seed of prosperity. With this practice, you can raise a great tree of prosperity. Then, under the shade of this tree, you can be relaxed, enjoy peace and contentment. This Rs. 1,000 can be used for developing your skills, upgrading your knowledge, or anything that you love to do, that which gives you inner peace and happiness. It could also be given in charity or spent on altruistic activities.

Your budget is your Defense Minister

Preparing a budget is of utmost importance. If we don't have a budget in place, then as soon as we get money, we might start shopping for our wants indiscriminately, thus indulging in unnecessary expenditure. Most often, we even fail to realize how money drains away. Hence many people are heard complaining, "We earn a lot, but we never understand where it disappears!"

Preparing a budget may reveal to us our extravagance and carelessness. Usually people are never alert in matters related to the budget. After making a budget, one realizes that even after taking care of all the necessary expenses, saving some money is easily possible. Additionally, we can make the desired donation to charity, thereby sowing the seeds of prosperity in life.

Budgeting helps save our higher aspirations from falling prey to petty desires. To fulfill our highest aspiration and highest purpose of life, we should avoid giving in to our petty desires. By documenting our budget, we can identify which desires can be fulfilled within the nine parts of our income.

After making ten parts of the income and keeping aside one part for ourselves, we can fit all other expenses in the remaining nine parts. We can use the expenses chart given in this chapter for reference. This exercise will help in accounting for all our bills and payments within the nine parts. We also can fit in whatever charity we want to make. Whatever we've been doing till date, can fit in our budget.

Your fortune

No more will it matter whether you make tens of thousands or a hundred. You have to make ten parts of your income even if you have only hundred rupees and give ten rupees to yourself. Taking those ten rupees, you can affirm, "This is my fortune; this is the seed for my prosperity." There's no need to doubt, "How can ten rupees be the seed for prosperity?" Even if doubts surface, you should still call it the seed for your tree of prosperity. This alone will open the road to abundance.

In many cases, people do not cultivate this habit, because their parents did not instill this habit in them. This is the reason they always feel short of money. Learn the secret of how to grow the great tree of prosperity as soon as possible. Start paying attention to your (and not the others') money today.

Even though money is a concrete path, it is not your destination. With the power of attention, attain wealth and let it pave a highway for you to reach your destination. Make money a boon; use it to reach your ultimate goal of permanent happiness, which can be attained only by realizing the Supreme Truth of life.

Exercise -

Write Down your income here (for example, Rs. 10,000/-): Amount: Rs._____/-

Reserve 1 part of 10 as your Seed of Prosperity (for example, Rs. 1000/-): Amount: Rs. _____/-

Prepare your budget by referring to the table of expense heads given earlier in this chapter (the percentages you allot to each expense head may vary).

Besides earning the wealth of money,
earn the wealth of love, attention, courage,
fearlessness, and health too.

3

Language and Definition of Money

When the Divine truth is associated with money,
then money becomes a gift of God.

Just as each one has a different definition of religion, deeds, success, and prosperity, the definition and understanding of money also differs.

A farmer was asked, "How is your work going on?" He said, "It's growing." That means his business is growing. This is the farmer's language. Just as crops and trees grow, so does his business.

A writer was posed with the same question, "How is your work going on?" He answered, "All right!" This is the writer's vocabulary. His 'all right!' corresponds to 'all write'.

An astrologer was asked, "How is your job going on?" He replied, "Way high, it's almost touching the stars."

"It's quite light!" was the response given by an electrician to the same question. Here light means easy-going, simple, not much. This is the electrician's vocabulary.

A tailor answered, "It's a bit tight!" Here tight means there are some difficulties in his work. These are the most *fitting* words a tailor may use.

A liftman's answer was, "It keeps going up and down." The liftman's lingo can explain the highs and lows of business in these words alone.

Just as each one has a different vocabulary, everyone uses different words for money according to their own dialect and lexicon. Different words lead to the formation of many right or wrong beliefs about money. Therefore, people discuss money frequently in many different ways according to their beliefs.

When two businessmen meet, they only talk about their business. Even if they are doing well in their business, you would find them saying, "There's some fluctuation going on, nowadays business is dull. These days, business is not what it used to be earlier." Such thinking is the main reason for attracting downswings and recession in business. Even when business is doing good, people do not say, "Everything is at its best." They are afraid that someone may cast an evil eye on their business and therefore don't express anything good about it.

People fail to understand that the words they speak gradually generate similar kind of feelings within them. Positive feelings attract money, while depression and worry about money actually diverts money away from their lives.

Hence, they should focus on harboring positive feelings and change the definition of money in their mind, "Money is meant for all, and is abundant. It is God's creativity, and is multiplying in my life." These words will have a positive impact on the feelings. After some time, they will notice positive results in their life. Positive feelings are like a magnet; they attract all the good things in life.

Henceforth, whenever you find yourself or someone around you saying, "There is no work, there's a recession," stop immediately. Tell yourself as well as the other person, "This thought itself might be the reason for recession. Our new thought can be the cause of recovery too." All you need to do is transmit just one new thought, "There wasn't much work earlier, but now I'm getting new opportunities." Or, "There *was* recession, but now business is flourishing." Or, "I had health problems earlier, but now my health is improving." Note that it does not matter whether others believe it or not, but at least you should make it a part of your life.

It is just that simple! This very thought can bring a huge revolution in your life. If you wish, this one thought can reach out to the universe. You can begin by passing on this thought to some people. Request them to pass it on to others.

You can change the world. The only requirement is that the chain of these positive thoughts should keep propagating, and the vocabulary and definition of money should change.

And to bring about this change let us also understand some delusions and myths related to money. Understanding these misconceptions and myths in the subsequent chapters will help us get rid of those beliefs and change our mindset towards prosperity and abundance.

Exercise-

Make a list of all the sentences that you frequently speak or think regarding money. Some common examples are:

1. Business is not doing well.
2. There is recession.

Some are masters of money.
Some have money as their master.

Three Delusions About Money

Don't deem money to be God or Devil
Don't squander it or hoard it
Don't run from it; instead, awaken!

Many people tend to nurse delusions about money. These misbeliefs further get converted into strong beliefs that manifest in their lives, eventually leading to problems.

Most people mainly harbor three types of delusions:

The first type believes that money alone is everything.

Some people believe money to be everything, and hence they hoard and hide money. For them, money is their God. People and relationships do not have much value in their eyes.

> Two friends were talking to each other on the telephone. In the middle of the conversation, one said, "I need Rs. 500." The other friend quickly replied, "It seems that there is some disturbance in the telephone line. I can't hear anything." The first friend repeated loudly, "I need

Rs. 500!" The other friend said, "Hello, hello… I can't hear anything; there is something wrong with the phone."

The telephone operator, who was listening to this conversation, said, "But, I can hear your friend clearly." The other friend said, "If you can hear him well, why don't you lend him the money?"

In this way, people develop hearing trouble when it comes to lending money, whereas they are all ears while receiving money. Such people don't want to hear about anything apart from money. Little do they know that the same money they hoard today may become the cause of their death!

A person won a lottery. The very same night, he was looted and murdered. So, is this incidence good or bad? Winning a lottery could have been such a wonderful turning point in his life. But the same lottery became the cause of his death.

Some people hide their money to the extent that they become misers. They focus all their thinking on finding unethical ways of earning money and then hoarding it. They are very alert about money matters but use their intelligence in the wrong direction.

A miser woke up one morning and found his wife dead. He immediately rushed to the kitchen and informed the cook to make breakfast for one person only. So, the first thought that came to him was avoiding the wastage of one person's breakfast. His mind worked at lightning speed for saving money but in a totally wrong direction.

A man went to buy bananas. He asked the shopkeeper, "How much for two bananas?" The shopkeeper said, "10 rupees." He picked up one banana and enquired further, "Fine, 10 for two. What if I buy one?" The shopkeeper answered, "6 rupees." Then, the person picked up one more banana and said, "The first banana costs 6 rupees, then the second would cost 4 rupees… together both cost 10 rupees. I want the second banana, which costs 4 rupees."

He thought so much on just a banana! Of course, this does not mean that one must thoughtlessly squander all money. Neither does it mean that one must accumulate and hoard as much money as possible.

One only needs to associate the right understanding of money. There is no need to hoard it nor squander it but use it appropriately. With this understanding, we can direct our thoughts in the right direction and strike the right balance between comforts and real happiness.

The second type considers money to be 'nothing.'

People who belong to this category, blow away their money. Money means nothing to them. Such people are careless and immature. They never reflect on the importance of money. Like the person who gave a beggar Rs. 100 and asked him how he had reached such a sorry state. The beggar replied, "I used to be very rich. Just like you, I, too, would give away money and ask questions to people. Continuing in this way, one day, I found myself in this poor state." This story shows how such people blow away money unnecessarily.

The third type runs away from money

Some people run away from money as if it were a serpent. They have wrong beliefs about money, which is why money is like a devil for them. They believe that even the touch of money will destroy their sanctity.

Therefore, neither consider money to be your God, nor the Devil. Neither squander money nor hoard it. Neither run away from it nor get overtly attached to it. Just awaken your understanding. Money is money; use it and forget it until the next need arises. Earn money and use it as a means to reach your destination.

After using a chair, you don't spend the whole day thinking about it. You think about it again only when you need it. Similarly, give the right place to money in your life – neither too high nor too low. You should use money; money should not use you. To master this art, let's reflect on some of the common myths about money in the next chapter.

Always work a bit more than what you're paid for.
Nature will then compensate the extra effort in abundance!

5

Thirteen Money Myths

One who has only money,
but no knowledge, understanding,
friends, relationships, or skills,
is indeed very poor.

Man's mind is like a pot of beliefs. At times, even after seeing the truth, the mind does not want to believe in it, while at times, it believes in notions without giving even a single thought to them. To break this pot of beliefs, let's shift our focus on the right understanding about money.

Mentioned below are thirteen common yet false beliefs regarding money. Let us take a look at them. You can then contemplate over these money myths and unearth the truth hidden behind them.

1. It is difficult to earn money.
2. People borrow money but never return it.
3. Money is God, or money is Devil.
4. Money is filth.
5. More money begets more problems.

6. With the arrival of money in our lives, friends turn into foes.
7. Money comes but never stays.
8. One who has a lot of money is less spiritual.
9. Itching in palms indicates that money is about to flow-in.
10. Those who earn a lot are rich.
11. I am nothing without money.
12. Money can buy everything.
13. Money, happiness, time, etc. are limited; we cannot share them with others.

Which of the above myths do you believe in?

When all money myths get busted, that's when you become truly prosperous.

We have myriad beliefs about money. But there is an important rule of nature: We find evidence for whatever we believe in. On finding evidence, beliefs become stronger. When our false beliefs become stronger, we find even stronger evidence. With stronger evidence, such false beliefs get deeply ingrained in our mind. This vicious cycle goes on, and beliefs become so entrenched that even though money keeps flowing in, so do problems.

This applies to all the beliefs related to money. Just because we believe in these myths, we get their evidence. Let's dig deeper at each of these money myths and try to unearth the truth.

1. It is difficult to earn money

Other related beliefs could be:

Earning money requires a lot of hard work.

No matter how hard we work, we will always remain poor.

The truth is money requires smart work. But when we keep repeating that it is difficult, it indeed becomes difficult. We need to re-affirm that money comes to us smoothly and easily. This definitely does not mean that we should go after easy money or earning money through illegal means. This only indicates that there is no need to repeat words like 'difficult' or 'hardship'. Thinking that earning money is difficult or requires a lot of hardship is a mindset that cuts us off from our real power. It is 'deficiency thinking'. These Deficiency Thoughts backfire. They attract incidents in our life, where we always have to keep working hard. Hence, we should repeat positive money affirmations that will bring positivity in life.

2. People borrow money but never return it

Not all people are the same. We make the mistake of distrusting people. By showing distrust towards others, we block the money coming towards us. With such thoughts, we stop wealth from flowing in our life. Instead, we should pray and bless people with the right mindset so that the flow keeps coming in everyone's lives.

3. Money is God, or money is Devil, or
4. Money is filth

For some, money is God; for some, it is the Devil; for some, it is filth. All these are false notions about money. Those, who regard money as filth, are wrong. So are people who consider money to be God or Devil. Money is just a neutral entity; it's a medium of exchange. People spread such misguided myths because of their ignorance or incomplete knowledge.

Money is neither good nor bad by itself. Money is like a knife in the kitchen. You never judge your knife to be good or bad. Nor do you say that the knife is filth. You just use it to cut vegetables or fruits, and keep it back in its place. You don't carry it around in your pocket. You are aware that it is nothing more than a tool. Similarly, money too is a tool and should be used appropriately rather than labeling it as good or bad.

5. More money begets more problems, or
6. With the arrival of money in our lives, friends turn into foes

Many people have this false belief that when money arrives in their lives, it creates problems and spoils their relationships. It turns friends into foes. The truth is that people are not trained to handle or manage money that's received suddenly and hence commit many mistakes. This becomes the cause of problems in their friendships and relationships. The real problem is not money, but the lack of training. Money is a tool. We need to get trained to be able to handle and use it effectively.

7. Money does come, but never stays

For some people, the problem is that money comes but disappears in no time. Understand the real reason which has fostered this belief. It is an understatement or rather wrong to say that the one who earns more is rich and the one who earns less is poor. One may earn a lot, but may not save at all, and spend it all. In fact, he is poor. Another person earns less but is able to retain the money, because of his habit of saving 10% of his income. In fact, rich people are those who can save, not those who earn more. 'More income means more money' is yet another myth. Hence, make it a habit to save with right understanding rather than the pursuit of earning more money.

8. One who has a lot of money is less spiritual

Another money myth is: 'Having more money means less spiritualism.' People believe that, 'If one earns more, they lose their focus on their inner journey.' This is because of the notion that if one pursues spiritualism, they may lose interest in earning money, thus reducing their wealth. But this is not the truth. With the understanding of true spirituality, one learns the right way to use money. They start respecting money and stop placing blocks in its flow. They no longer feel the sense of ownership about money and are liberated from attachment to money. Real spirituality shifts them from being a mere watchman of money to being a master of money.

9. Itching in palms indicates that money is about to flow in

Some of us believe that an itching sensation in the palms is a sure sign that we will receive money through some means. Let us understand the fact behind this belief. We do most of our work using our hands and palms. Earning money is an activity associated with labor of hands. When hardworking hands are empty with nothing to do, an unpleasant sensation is felt in them, which is perceived by some as an itching sensation. Such hands wish to begin some work immediately. Money is bound to flow in with work. And that's how this belief has come into being.

In ancient times, most of the work was done using hands as there were no machines. But in today's world, manual labor has reduced. Such a sensation can be experienced by only those whose hands are used to a lot of hard manual work. This belief was apt in olden days, but could be irrelevant today. Hence, it is important to understand the basis of such beliefs and not let them become a noose around the neck.

10. **Those who earn a lot are rich, or**

11. **Money can buy everything**

Money cannot buy everything, because love, true happiness, and fulfillment are achieved through inner development; not with money. The poorest of all is the one who has nothing else but money. Money is not the only wealth in life. One should acquire many other higher treasures in life such as love, time, attention, and knowledge. Along with money, one must learn to achieve the lucrative capital of love, the asset of attention, the treasure of time, the fortune of fearlessness, and the wealth of health. Nothing can be of greater value than this in life.

12. **I am nothing without money**

Complete knowledge imparts the understanding that money is a path, not the destination. We are supposed to reach somewhere, using money. Pause for a moment and contemplate on the question: "In my life, do I consider money to be the path or the destination?" A path is something that we use to reach somewhere. Considering money to be the destination means taking money to be the ultimate goal of life. Money is the means, not the end.

13. Money, happiness, time, etc. are limited; we cannot share them with others

The feeling of ownership (obsession) with money turns you into its slave. Let go of this feeling. Praying to God, "I submit my body, mind, and wealth to you," would mean submitting the sense of ownership. The sense of ownership is a cause of sorrow. Many have ruled on earth, but no one has ever been the permanent master of its wealth and treasures. With the desire for ownership, we invite suffering in our lives. This feeling of ownership induces the worry about money. Hence, it is essential to attain liberation from this feeling.

We put so many limitations around us, such as, "This is mine, That's yours. This is my country, That is your country, This is my tree, That is your tree," and so on. Such limitations give rise to problems. By repeating such sentences, everything seems to be deficient, even though everything is actually abundant. If we share all the produce in this world, no one will ever fall short of food. The tendency of having ownership of everything should stop. God has created everything in abundance; we only need to identify our needs and fulfill each other's needs by coming together and sharing.

Ask yourself honestly, "What is my real goal? What is the purpose of my life?" Those who feel money is just a means and not the goal should work towards reaching their actual goal. Those who are not yet convinced about this should contemplate more on the above question; because this will prove to be one of the most important decisions of your life.

Use money with the understanding given in this chapter. There is no need to believe myths like: "Money is just the filth in my hands, money is God or Devil, money is the problem, and so on…" You simply need to start using money with the right understanding.

Now that we are clear about money myths, let's understand how money flows.

Exercise-

Write down all such beliefs about money that you may have heard. Now contemplate on the right understanding that needs to be harbored instead of these beliefs.

Blood and money are alike.
Both should keep flowing uninterrupted

6

Let Money Flow

*The smoothest way of transacting money is:
Give with one hand and take with the other!*

Flowing water is fresh while stagnant water stinks. Similarly, when money flows it remains fresh. Stagnant money is just like stagnant water.

The flow of money stops in the lives of those who repress and hide money, as well as those who are unable to think about money at all.

The flow of money does not entail just spending it. It means spending money on endeavors that multiply money or buying things that help in your own development. With development, money too starts growing automatically. When this happens, then the circle of money flow is complete.

The flow of money should not be mistaken as 'money gone, will never return'. In fact, such money returns in multiples. It is a law of nature: **Whatever you give, comes back to you in multiples.** This alone completes the circuit.

If you observe carefully, you will realize that this law operates in every aspect of life. Till date, whatever you have given has come back to you. If you have given appreciation, then you too have been appreciated in return. If you have showered love on others, then you too have received love. If you have helped others, then you too received help in times of need. When you prayed for others, you too received its benefit. If someone throws abuses at others, he surely gets abuses in return.

When we call out at the 'echo point' in the mountains, our own voice echoes back. When we throw a boomerang in the air, it flies right back at us. Such is the law of nature: **Whatever we give, is exactly what we will get.** If we propagate happy thoughts, then the same happy thoughts return to us. This is how life works—whether we believe it or not. Nature's laws do not depend upon our beliefs, they are simply the truth.

Hence, we should awaken to knowledge. Everything is flowing in our life. When we are not aware of this truth and receptive to the flow, those things do not reach us. It is now time to awaken and shed away our inertia to acquire whatever is waiting to flow in our life. On awakening, we will notice that money problems have persisted because we have not paid attention to small but important details. If we follow practices like making a budget, keeping aside one part of our income for ourselves, following the rule of money flow, then our financial problems will vanish.

Let us take an example to learn how effective the flow of money proves to be.

> There was a bazaar with various kinds of shops. Every day, the shopkeepers would open their shops at the right time and begin their business. One day, it so happened that not a single customer visited this bazaar. Everyone was just staring at each other's face. All of them were in a fix. Suddenly a thought occurred to one of the shopkeepers. He got up, entered the neighboring shop, and bought some items for himself. The neighboring shopkeeper thus had some business. He too thought,

'Why not buy something for my family?' He then went to some other shop and bought something for his family. Thus, all the shopkeepers bought something from one another. So, without getting even a single customer, the flow of money took place, and each one gave and also received money. As a result, the money circuit was completed, and everyone was happy.

Progress gets stunted in society when money stops flowing. The society in which money circulates, makes progress in leaps and bounds. Those who understand this law, make the right use of money. Those who do not know this law live in fear of losing money, and thus end up playing the role of a watchman to their money. We shall understand more about this in the next chapter.

If all the fruits available in the world are distributed
then there won't be dearth of food for anyone.
God has created everything in abundance.
Let us get rid of all fear and greed,
and get together to share everything
and fulfill everyone's needs.

Be the Owner of Money, Not its Caretaker

One who can give is the owner.
One who cannot give is
merely playing the role of a caretaker.

A person is walking on the road, holding the rope tied to a bull. Is this person the bull's master? Or is the bull the master? To find the answer, you just need to cut the rope and watch what happens! Who chases whom? Does the bull run after the person, or does the person run after the bull? The answer is quite simple; the person runs after the bull. On similar lines, some people are masters of money, while some have money as their master.

Once upon a time, a king heard about a miser living in his kingdom. The king announced that the greatest miser would be rewarded with half the king's wealth. This miser participated in the contest and won. The king called in the miser and told him, "Half my wealth is yours. But how can you take so much wealth to your house? You will have to build a new place to keep so much wealth. That will cost a lot of money. Instead, bring all your wealth, keep it along with mine, and take care of the entire treasury. Whenever I need money, I would use it from my share. You, in turn, will get a readymade safe vault." The miser was overjoyed. He brought in and added his wealth to the king's treasure.

The chief minister asked the king, "Your Highness, why have you done this? Why have you handed over the entire treasure to the miser?!"

The king revealed the secret, "Yes, I have handed over the entire treasure to the miser. Whenever we need money, we will take it from my share of wealth. How long would this miser live anyway? We need a good caretaker for the royal treasury, and this miser is the best person for this job. He will not spend a single penny. You think that I have given half my wealth to him, but that's not so. In fact, we have got a caretaker who will work for free. Otherwise, we would have to pay a guard for taking care of the treasury, as well as keep a watch on his integrity, lest he gets tempted to steal. Now that's not the case with the miser. Additionally, he will stay awake all night and checks intermittently fearing, that his treasure will be stolen. We have got such a good caretaker free of cost!"

With this story, we learn that only the owner can give money; a caretaker merely takes care of it. For instance, if someone gave you a pen and asked you to take care of it, then you cannot give it to anyone else because you do not own that pen. But if it was your own pen, then you can give it to anyone you wish. This brings us to another important point i.e., **One who can give is the owner, while one who cannot give is merely a caretaker.**

Contemplate on this for a while: Are you the owner of your own life or its caretaker? If you live your life for others, you are its owner.

Only that, which you give, leads to your progress.

Whatever you take merely helps in your sustenance.

The great law of nature related to money matters is: 'That which you give benefits you.' Whatever you give to others, e.g., time, money, help, love, attention, appreciation, food, knowledge, all that results in your progress. While whatever you take merely helps in your sustenance.

Logically man thinks that only taking something will help in his progress. But the law of nature states, 'Whatever you give, alone helps in your progress; that alone proves to be beneficial for you.' Initially, you may find this illogical and unacceptable. But once you put it into practice, the truth will be evident. In fact, you may have already used this law unknowingly. Whatever you have given till date has helped you progress physically, mentally, socially, financially, and spiritually. The law of nature also states: **You can give only that which nature has deposited in your custody.** Whenever you give something, it will return to you multifold.

Money is not the sole form of wealth on this earth. No one can become wealthy with just the wealth of money. Apart from money, there are many other types of wealth such as love, attention, courage, fearlessness, health, etc. Man is endowed with all these types of wealth. If man does not earn the wealth of love, attention, time, and courage, and is focused on accumulating only the wealth of money; he repents miserably at the end of his life. Therefore, now onwards, along with earning money, we need to learn the secret of earning the lucrative capital of love, the asset of attention, the treasure of time, the fortune of fearlessness, and the wealth of health.

This law of nature tells us exactly how money can flow in our life. Once we apply this rule, money will grow in our life and we can achieve complete development in all facets of life.

According to this law, if you think on what you possess that you can give, you will find that you have love, time, attention, money, and the feeling of giving. Whatever amount of these types of wealth you have, they need to be shared in the right proportion. Then nature will give back to you multifold, for you to share them again. This is how you can enjoy the self-expression of abundance in life.

Before applying this law of nature, you need to also understand what nature has deposited in your care? What should you give? Whom should you give? Who are you? Who is the giver?

Money is a means for things that come in your life. Money helps in the give-and-take of goods. In ancient times, people used to barter wheat with rice. They had to carry sacks of grain to make such deals. In modern times, people use money instead of grain. Money has made commercial exchange convenient and easy. That's the purpose of money—to make transactions simple and convenient. But people have forgotten this purpose of money and made it a goal in itself.

But it's time to gain understanding about money and apply this important law of nature to bring about our own as well as others' progress.

After understanding the profundity of this law of nature, we can easily give when someone asks for something—be it charity, co-operation, assistance, time, love, attention, or money. All that we give brings the feeling of fulfillment. We will easily be able to make donations of money too, provided we have made a budget and have also documented it.

If we keep working diligently to achieve abundance with full faith and regularity, irrigating it with savings, then soon it will grow up to become a giant tree of prosperity. Under the shade of this tree, we can then meditate, enjoy, and rest, as well as become an inspiration for others to walk on the path of true prosperity.

With this understanding, as we become the owner of our life, and allow money to flow, let us also understand how we can avoid placing blocks in this flow.

8

Do Not Block Money

One who despises and envies rich people;
can never become rich.

The biggest block in the flow of money is worry. When thoughts about money cause worry, those thoughts become a block in the flow of money.

It is essential for money to flow. Blockage in the flow of money is as harmful as a blood clot which stops the flow of blood. In our body, as the blood flows, it gets purified and cleansed. But, a small clot adversely affects the blood circulation, impacting the physiology. It can lead to fatal diseases like a stroke or a heart attack.

So it is with money. Even a small pebble can block the flow of money. *Blood and money are very similar – both need to keep flowing.* The stinginess of a miser is like a block, a clot that obstructs the flow of money.

Suppose that you have turned on the radio and tuned it to a music station. Someone else barges in, fiddles with the knobs, and then starts complaining, "Why is the music not coming on?" What would you tell the person? You would tell him that the radio was already tuned. He fiddled with the controls and the radio got mistuned. In the same manner, money is always flowing towards everyone. But people mistune the frequency by unknowingly placing blocks in the flow of money.

Here are some examples to show the kind of blocks one places in the flow of money.

- A person told his friend, "Today I visited a shop and paid Rs. 50 to the shopkeeper. He thought that I had given him Rs. 100. So he gave me goods worth Rs. 40 and returned Rs. 60. I immediately slipped out of the shop before he could realize it." Now this slippage is that small pebble, which would block the flow of money in his future.

- A bus passenger happily informed, "The bus arrived at my stop before the bus conductor could approach me for the ticket. So I got out of the bus and saved ten rupees." This means that the passenger has placed a block of Rs. 10 in his life. He is not aware whether this block of Rs. 10 will stop Rs. 1,000 or Rs. 10,000 from coming in his life. Even a small pebble can cause a major blockage.

- A boy was bragging to his friends, "I went for a movie yesterday. The clerk at the ticket counter gave me two tickets by mistake. I sold off one ticket and bought some snacks with that money. I enjoyed it!"

- A person met with a major loss in his business. His outstanding debt amounted to millions of rupees. His lawyer advised him, "If you pay me just Rs. 50,000, I will fight your case and free you from all your debts." The businessman replied, "No, I will not do that. I have taken money from people, and I will repay the debts. By paying you Rs. 50,000, I may be acquitted from the debts. But, the fact is that I have taken money from them, and I do not want to place any blocks in the flow of money." After some time, this businessman was able to pay off all his debts. This could happen because he had the right understanding of money. Had the businessman accepted the lawyer's offer, he would have been acquitted but would have created a huge money block for his future.

- A student narrated his problem, "Some months back, I helped a friend by loaning him Rs. 20,000. Now, I am asking him for the money, but he refuses to pay me back. I have been visiting him frequently since the last four months but to no effect."

    He was asked to state this request to his friend in a particular way. He did that. But his friend still did not pay the money back. He tried all different ways that were suggested to him for recovering his amount. But all in vain.

    Then the student was asked whether he had ever taken money from someone and not repaid it. The student reflected on it and remembered that he had not paid some part of the fees for a course he had attended. He was advised to settle the fees in instalments, even if it meant starting with just fifty rupees. This repayment would serve as an indication to nature that he did not intend to hold back anyone's money; that he was prepared to give. Only then this circuit would be completed.

Money never flows one way alone; it needs to flow in both directions. If we have blocked someone's money, then money that flows towards us gets blocked too. Even a small step in the right direction can bring great results.

When the student began to repay his debt, to his surprise, his friend, too, called to inform him that he would repay his money by the first week of next month.

A little experiment tried by this student resulted in the removal of the money block. He had held back someone else's money in the past, but as he started paying it little by little, the results showed up immediately. This signifies that when we block others' money, our money gets blocked too. This is an irrefutable law of nature.

We, too, need to work on these principles. Let us avoid introducing any such money blocks in our own lives. If we have already done that by mistake, then right from today, we need to stop it. Even a small pebble hampers the pipeline and reduces the flow of water. In the same way, even a small money block can stop the inflow of money.

Remove even the tiniest money block from your money pipeline and thereby give the right direction and purpose to the flow of money.

Contemplate on any such blocks that you may have placed in the flow of money, knowingly or unknowingly.

1. _____
2. _____
3. _____
4. _____

Set the Right Aim for Earning Money

*No aim can be achieved,
until you decide its timeline.*

Having understood the importance of clearing our past money blocks, the next step is to set a goal and work towards achieving that goal. To make the most of our life and attain what we truly desire, setting an aim is imperative.

Setting an aim helps us to stay focused. It gives us the required strength and willpower to strive towards achieving that aim. It gives us a vision and motivation that helps us become more organized in life. So it is with earning money as well. Setting the right aim makes us more focused, organized, and independent, leading us towards financial peace and freedom.

But how do we know if we have decided the right aim? Here are the steps to set the right aim for earning money. Aligning ourselves to that aim can help achieve it in no time.

First step: Set a positive aim

The first step in setting an aim is to not just set any aim, but to set a positive aim for yourself. For instance, "I will start saving money to buy my own house" is a positive aim. While something like, "I won't spend a single penny as I need to buy a house" is a negative aim. As you start focusing on the positive aspects, you will automatically stop indulging in unwarranted expenses. This happens because your attention gets focused on your aim. In fact, you won't even notice when you stopped squandering your money.

Second step: Set the timeline for realizing your aim

An aim cannot be called an aim unless you set a timeline for it. Once you set a date for the attainment of your aim, focus entirely on achieving it. And even if you are not successful in achieving it, do not get dejected or let go of your aim. Also, ensure not to set such a distant timeline that it feels meaningless. For example, "Before dying, I want to be free of all my debts" is an aim that does not make sense as it does not have a practical timeline. Even if you did achieve it just before death, when will you enjoy the happiness of having achieved your aim? You can decide an aim to earn X amount in 1 year or 5 years, and so on.

Third step: Write down your aim

Until you see your aim in front of your eyes, it does not turn into reality. So write down your aim and stick it at places where you can be reminded. For example: you can stick it in your bathroom, or on the mirror, on the refrigerator door, or on the steering wheel of your car. It can be the screensaver or wallpaper on your mobile or laptop, and so on. In this way, keeping your aim before your eyes at all times will help you to focus on it constantly.

Fourth step: Concentrate on your aim with full focus

Always keep your aim in front of your eyes. If you aim to buy a house, make its blueprint. Read magazines on houses, cultivating a garden, architecture, and other related topics. Create a blueprint of the home you would like to own. Immerse yourself so much in your aim that your superfluous expenses will automatically stop. Then you won't have to remind yourself time and again about not spending unnecessarily; instead, you will always remember that you have set aside your funds for a particular purpose.

Focus on the benefits that you will get once you achieve your aim, not on the sacrifices you make to reach there. If you are unable to focus on the benefits of achieving the aim, then in all probability, you will not be able to achieve it. And even if you somehow do manage to achieve it, you won't be able to sustain it.

Keep these four steps in your mind. These four simple steps can also free you from all your debts. All you have to do is follow the simple tips provided in this chapter.

To attain your aim, set a timeline for it, write down that date, and focus on it. On doing this, you will be amazed to see money flowing towards you to help realize your aim.

Your budget is your defense minister.
It saves your higher aspirations from your petty desires.

10

Focus on What is Gained, Not on What is Spent

*Whatever you give
certainly comes back to you, in multiples.*

As we decide an aim and work towards achieving it, we should also learn the art of verbalizing what we've gained rather than what has been spent.

We usually hear people say, "Today I spent 100 rupees," "Today 1,000 rupees have gone from my wallet." Most people can be seen speaking in this manner after shopping or buying something. This gives a negative twist to the story. You did give away Rs. 100, but you surely bought something in exchange for that amount. We need to learn to start talking about what we've gained in exchange for that money. It could be anything—a shirt, a purse, a bicycle, or a book.

Unfortunately, no one talks about what was purchased. The tongue is habituated to always seek the missing tooth, despite having the rest of the teeth intact. Likewise, we usually mention what is gone and are more bothered about it, while we never mention 'what is there' or 'what has come'. This negative thinking goes on, leading to depletion of money.

We get so many things in exchange for money, but this negative thinking that 'money has gone away' has to stop. Let us stop telling ourselves half the truth, let us say the complete truth.

Let's not complain by making statements like, "Money never stays. No sooner do I get change for a 500 rupee note, it gets spent within no time." Instead of complaining, we can say, "With Rs. 500, I filled petrol, I could travel comfortably. I purchased grocery, etc." This will give the right direction to our focus. It does not mean that we should become spendthrifts and squander all the money. We need to follow the middle path and use money without falling prey to extremes.

From now on, whenever you buy something, don't tell half the truth to yourself or to others. State the complete truth, "I spent this much money, and these are the things that I bought." If you take a taxi and then lament that so much money was spent, you need to stop making such statements. You did spend the money, but you received its benefits too – like you could avoid standing in the long bus queue, in the scorching heat, as well as save your time."

If, after buying a book, you say, "Today I spent Rs. 100," correct yourself, saying, "Today I got this book for Rs. 100."

Our subconscious mind works according to the information we pass on to it. When we keep lamenting, "This is gone... that too is gone..." then we are giving a wrong signal to our subconscious mind that "I always keep losing," and that is what manifests in our life. When someone says, "I got this... I have received that today..." his subconscious mind attracts those things. According to the law of nature, focusing on scarcity and loss leads to further scarcity of money. Hence, we need to shift our focus on abundance.

Such thoughts are feelings related to money. Money is not the problem; the feelings and thoughts that we harbor about money is the real problem. If we associate the feeling of lack with money and keep prompting, "This much money is gone... that much has been spent…", then we experience deprivation of wealth even though it is abundant.

Hence, whenever we purchase something, we should tell ourselves what we have gained by spending that money. By doing so, we will attract abundance in our life. This brings us to another technique related to purchases that we should keep in mind while we learn the art of right verbalization. Let us discuss this technique in the next chapter.

Use Money for Needs, Not for Wants

*If you make purchases on special occasions
by looking at what others have,
then those very occasions lead to financial problems.*

Very often, man invites misery in his life by fulfilling his wants while ignoring his essential needs. The reason for such erratic behavior is the copycat tendency or, the habit of comparison.

In simple terms, copycat behavior is where a person keeps comparing himself with others and tries to match them. He wants to buy or have those things that others have. He continuously keeps thinking, "Why do I have less than the other person?" Many people purchase goods only because they see others having them. They end up procuring even absolutely unnecessary items. At such times, one should ask oneself, "Is this really what I need or do I want it because someone else has it?"

This brings us to a very important aspect of money, that of **Need and Want.**

A Need denotes something that you really require, without which you cannot do and cannot survive or make progress. Need is different from want.

A Want is something that the mind has become fond of, or the urge to buy it because someone else has bought it. Comparing with others, people make purchases that are unnecessary then.

It is a simple technique of asking ourselves, "Is this a Need or a Want? N or W?", while buying anything. This simple question can save us from many financial troubles. If the answer is 'W' (Want), then ask the next question, "Have I already fulfilled all my needs like children's expenses, books, medicines for family members, etc.?" If the answer is 'No,' then we must make sure that we fulfill the needs first. This does not mean that wants should never be attended to. But first, we should take care of our needs before moving onto wants.

You will be surprised to see more than half of your money problems getting resolved just by asking this simple question, "N or W?"

When you ask yourself honestly, "Am I buying this because my neighbor has bought it? Or am I buying it after making provision for all my needs?" You will definitely get the answer from within. Probably your neighbor has already fulfilled all his needs and is therefore now indulging in his wants. But you should shift to your wants only when you are through with your needs. This is how you can hush up the copycat of comparison. Asking the question "N or W?" shuts its mouth.

On the occasions of festivals and marriages, people spend a lot without discretion, just because others tell them to or because they see others doing it. The question "N or W?" makes us alert even during such events.

In this way, just a simple but straightforward question, "N or W?" can awaken us. Let none of our decisions happen in ignorance. If on a special occasion, our purchases are being influenced by others, then this habit could lead to bankruptcy instead of celebration.

People blow away their money by trying to imitate others. We should never let this happen with us.

> A student was returning to India from overseas. He knew this technique. Friends and relatives of those returning from overseas expect to receive various goodies like music systems, iPhones, clothes, or some valuable items that are cheaply available there.
>
> When this student went out shopping in that country, he remembered this phrase: "Is this my Need or Want?" While shopping, he was able to question himself for every purchase and avoid buying things that were mere wants. He still feels happy about the right decision he made at that time.

Inculcate this little habit in your nature: Before doing anything or before purchasing anything, just ask yourself, "Is it N or W? Need or Want?" If it is a need, then go ahead and procure it. But if it is a want, then stop right there. In future, you will pat your back saying, "It's good that I took the right decision at the right time and saved so much money. Otherwise, without awareness, I was making so many unnecessary purchases." Once your needs are fulfilled, you can attend to wants too but with a relaxed mindset that all your needs are taken care of.

Applying this mantra protects our highest desire from falling prey to measly wishes. At the end of their lives, people lament, "I always had a higher desire but I was neither able to spare time nor money for it. My highest wish remains unfulfilled." Often, man can make significant sacrifices very easily, but cannot remain alert when smaller wants arise. Trying to fulfill all his minor wants, he remains devoid of his supreme goal.

You have to decide which of your desires you want to fulfill. Some desires emanate from the personal ego, while some arise from the Self (the Inner Truth). With your defense minister Mr. Budget by your side, you can fulfill your desires within the nine parts of your income. All your N expenses (needs) can fit into the nine parts of your budget. Just as people with good time management skills complete all their tasks within a given time, similarly, all the needs can be fulfilled within the available money.

There is enough money available for fulfilling needs, but it always falls short when it comes to satisfying greed. Greed has no limit. Initially, you might find it difficult to apply the 'N or W' technique. But gradually, you will find that it is possible to do this.

Exercise-

Make a list of occasions in your life where you tend to indulge in your wants. Apply this N or W technique for those occasions.

Each drop of water helps to fill the lake.
So do not consider even a small saving to be trivial.

12

Lack of Money or Right Thinking?

There is no money problem,
there is only 'idea' problem.

Let money grow in your life; but let it not lead you away from the spiritual path. Instead, it should help you attain the real purpose of life.

If you regard money as your only goal in life, then money will be of no help to you. But if you consider money as a means, it can help you in a big way. When money becomes a goal, your emotions get attached to it; it becomes a craving. Let us not be emotionally attached to money.

By getting emotionally attached to money, people cannot think clearly or generate new creative ideas. Therefore, it is of utmost importance to understand that:

Money is never the problem; emotions are the problem. Lack of money is not the problem, lack of ideas is the problem.

Always remember this statement because new ideas are often not easily understood or accepted by people. Haven't we sensed a dire need for new and unique creations all around us? If someone can fulfill this need with new inventions, if someone can present and offer these innovations to the masses, there will never be any dearth of money.

In today's fast-paced world, very few have the time and readiness to think on new aspects because the art of thinking out-of-box is rarely taught in schools. If our educational system had helped us master this art, then there would neither be any money problems nor the need to lead a miserly life. This is because we would then have developed confidence in our abilities to create healthy opportunities for earning money.

We can fulfill people's needs through innovation—needs, which people themselves are unaware of. The world is changing rapidly and everyone is looking out for new ideas and inventions. With such creations, one can never fall short of money.

A miser is not confident of his own abilities

A miser is always "miser-able" and makes his family life miserable too. This is because he is not confident of his capability of earning money. A miser keeps worrying about how he can earn more money when his existing funds will be exhausted. Instead of developing his abilities, he relies on luck. He believes in the play of fate and indulges in lotteries, and hence he does not develop his earning ability.

People who have developed the capability of earning money are always at ease. They are confident that whenever the need for money arises, they can think of new ideas. They are aware of the fact that lack of money is not the problem; lack of ideas is the problem.

Recognize the opportunity and get lucky

People lack the training on how to think; hence they get bogged down by limited thinking. With the right training, their abilities can be enhanced. Here, enhancing one's abilities implies learning new skills, learning new technologies or arts, upgrading one's knowledge, understanding and applying new thinking strategies.

Even contemplating on how to provide better services in our chosen field of work leads to strengthening of our capability. Strengthening our abilities alone will beget money. Therefore, we should leave our fate to itself and instead focus on boosting our capability and capacity.

To boost our capability, we need to awaken our inner wisdom, and learn the art of making decisions. We need to be alert about identifying opportunities because good luck follows opportunities. We shouldn't miss a single chance of making the right decisions, getting rid of laziness, and disciplining the mind. We have to make the most of every opportunity.

Many just keep complaining, "How lucky that person is! He has so much money. I alone am unlucky." The fact is that the one who can recognize an opportunity is lucky. The one who can overcome inertia, generate and save money at the right time, is lucky. Otherwise, postponing or remaining ignorant of these activities only leads to regret because a large amount of time is wasted in procrastination.

To try their luck, many people fall into the trap of gambling and lotteries. As a result, they waste their time as well as money. They get entangled in baseless schemes that assure unrealistic returns in a very short term. We should never get allured by such schemes, because they only lead to repentance.

Money is a boon; don't turn it into a bane

While preparing your budget, focus on the right sections. If you have planned well, you will see that everything else fits smoothly into your budget.

Money is God's creation; it is a highly creative system. Consider how all activities happen in this world and how billions of people transact so easily... isn't this a fantastic arrangement?! Money has been created with the sole purpose of simplifying the process of give-and-take in this world. With this understanding, we should make money a blessing and not a curse.

Some people let money get to their heads. They become egoistic. This way, the boon turns into a bane for them. Hence, we should always be careful not to let money become a curse. The habit of being arrogant on gaining wealth and then insulting or hurting others leads to dire consequences.

How to pay off your debts

Staying clear of all the pitfalls mentioned earlier, you also need to clear off your debts, if any.

As mentioned in the earlier chapter, debts are also one of the reasons for creation of blocks in the flow of money. One needs to avoid such money blocks by paying off debts on time.

If you have borrowed money, then you need to ensure that you repay that debt. For any reason, if you cannot return the debt immediately, then you ought to inform the lender about it. This boosts your trustworthiness. People will be prepared to help you in the future only when you convey your earnest desire to repay past debt.

If you are unable to repay your debt within the committed time, you can assure the lender by saying, "I sincerely want to repay you; please grant me a little more time and encouragement. I have heard and read about such guidance on money, which has prompted me to pay off all my loans. I do not want to create any money blocks in my life by not repaying this debt. I need your help in this regard. I am going to save some money from my income to pay back your money on priority." These words can reassure the lender. On the contrary, if you avoid communicating with your lender, he might lose all hopes of recovering his money and you will lose his trust.

When the borrower makes a genuine request of wanting to repay his debts, people will support him. Perhaps they may even lend additional capital to help him progress in his field of work. Those who have taken such a courageous and upright stand in their lives have worked hard with honesty and gained freedom by paying off their loans.

In this way, you can also inspire others to be free from debt. With strong determination and perseverance, you can increase your earning ability and achieve every success.

Exercise-

Contemplate on the skills that you can enhance and write them down. This could include enrolling yourself for webinars or training courses to help upgrade your knowledge, and so on.

*Money will come to you
only when you increase your capabilities.
Hence, leave your destiny to itself,
and work on developing your capacity and capability.*

13

Learning How to Learn

*Besides earning money, also learn to earn
the lucrative capital of love, the asset of attention,
the treasure of time, the fortune of fearlessness,
and the wealth of good health.*

What is the most valuable asset we possess? Even if we don't have loads of wealth, we still possess the most valuable asset—the ability to learn. It is this ability due to which we can augment our knowledge and harness our talents. We have to use this ability to get appropriate returns.

The knowledge that we gain through education, work experience, training, etc. contributes to elevate our earning ability. Studies show that many wealthy people had humble beginnings, very often going through setbacks. They then used their valuable time and hard work to enhance their learning capabilities. We too can do this. We can start enhancing our learning abilities today itself, or at least decide a date today and begin on that date.

A learned person, in the true sense, is one who has learned how to keep continuously learning throughout. Learning is a journey that goes on till the very end of our life. We learn to drive, to use technology, to cook, speak a new language, whistle, write stories, play a musical instrument, play a sport. But has it ever occurred to us that we should also learn how to learn. Have we ever given a thought that learning how to learn is something worthwhile? Learning is an art too.

If we wish to achieve our goal within a short time, it is very important to learn how to learn. It is only when we start learning 'how to learn' that we begin to appreciate the art of learning. For this, we need right thinking, higher awareness, and deep contemplation. We need to inculcate the habit of improving upon whatever we have already learnt. To learn anything, we need practice. This habit can make us an expert in our chosen field. After learning the art of learning, we will take lesser time to learn other things in life. If learning the 'art of learning' can save us so much time, then we should invest time in learning this art.

With regular practice, listening, reading, contemplation, and application, we can become an expert learner, thereby strengthening our capabilities. Old age has nothing to do with physical age. We start ageing when we stop learning. We can keep learning something new till the last day of our physical life. Not only does this practice delay our ageing, but also enables us to accomplish amazing work in our lives, thus setting an example for others.

> There was a great wrestler named Ramamurti. He used to place a wooden plank on his chest and get an elephant to stand on it. People used to be astounded with his strength. But Ramamurti was very weak as a child. He would perennially fall ill and easily get tired. But he did not remain a victim of his weakness for long. While he was a child, he decided that he will not continue to be a weakling, but rather set an example of strength. His resoluteness bore fruit.
>
> Today, the world remembers Ramamurti as an example of success and strength. When Ramamurti was asked about the secret of his success, he said: "Regular training

can strengthen even the weakest of bodies. During this training, you should lift only as much weight as you can. But lift this weight several times a day. Gradually keep increasing the weight. Soon, your body can be as strong as steel!"

We can draw inspiration from this secret disclosed by Ramamurti to develop ourselves in every type of art, to achieve success, and to boost our capabilities.

There is a story of a shepherd that is similar to the story of Ramamurti:

> The shepherd used to tend cows and sheep. Every day, he used to visit a temple on a hill to offer his prayers. He would begin his work only after this prayer.
>
> One day, one of his cows gave birth to a calf. From that day onwards, he started carrying the calf on his shoulders to the temple. Gradually, the growing calf's weight started increasing, and so did the shepherd's strength. The shepherd was unaware that his strength had increased so much.
>
> With the passage of time the young calf turned into a full-grown bull. As was his routine, the shepherd continued to lift this bull on his shoulders every morning and visit the temple on the hill! People were astounded to see his herculean act. They would line up by the sides of the road to witness this amazing act every morning. The bull, too, got used to the habit of sitting on the shepherd's shoulders, just as the shepherd got used to lifting the bull's weight. So, this was a casual routine for them, while for others, it was next to impossible.

This amusing example of the shepherd emphasizes the practice of gradually increasing our abilities. **Practice daily, do only as much as you can, but do it as many times as you can.** With this mantra of practice, nothing is impossible.

If you ask successful artists their secret of success, they will share that along with other factors, the most important factor was continuous practice. The world-renowned magician, P.C. Sorcar, was asked, "What is the secret of your amazing magic?" The magician quoted three secrets for his success. "First: Practice, Second: Practice, and Third: Practice." With this answer, he underlined the importance of practice to the world. If any one person in this world can accomplish a certain task, then we too can learn and accomplish the same, with discipline, right training, and persistent practice.

The more and the faster we learn, the quicker is our professional progress, and the higher we climb up the ladder of success. With this, we can move ahead in all aspects of our life. Learners always equip themselves with additional information. This additional information helps solve any upcoming problems and get desired results. The more knowledge we gather, the greater is the freedom and opportunities that come our way.

There is always a gap between where we are now and where we want to be. But sure enough, we can bridge this gap with the right knowledge and skill. What got us till where we are today need not lead us to where we want to be. Hence, we need to keep learning something new and different that aligns with our chosen goal. We need to embrace new technology and creative methods. We need to practice all of these abundantly.

By developing and applying the art of learning, we can grow in every sphere of our life. We can become more capable of supporting our family and helping our friends in enhancing their abilities too.

But here is a word of caution: We should never make the mistake of comparing ourselves with others. Comparison does not help; instead, it harms. One should be aware of thoughts such as, 'He earns so much, and I earn so less...' We should take inspiration from others rather than comparing ourselves with them. We can surely compare where we stand today with where we were in the past. We can compete with ourselves and analyze our present state, situation, system, strength, and abilities. Unless we are aware of our current state, we cannot learn how to learn.

It is essential to analyze where you stand today. Which challenges are cakewalks for you, while which ones seem impossible? Do you wake up every morning at the decided time, or do you tend to oversleep the morning alarm? Are you overweight or are you working towards becoming healthier? Do you have any vices such as consuming excess tea, coffee, binge-watching television, binging on food, smoking, drinking, etc. that you want to let go off, but aren't able to? Are your house and office space systematically arranged and clean? Have you identified your time killers? How often do you fulfil your commitments? In a day, how long can you work with total concentration? Have you worked towards letting go of any of your bad habits and tried to inculcate new healthy ones? Are you reading this book after thoughtful consideration, or just because you happened to come across it? Are you aware of how you would spend your day tomorrow?

You can introspect on such questions and begin to train yourself, right from today.

Begin the task of introspection today. Identify your strengths and opportunities for improvement and decide the necessary action plan to train yourself. This training will not only make you successful but also help you in attaining the ultimate purpose of life.

May money increase in your life
but let it not lead you away from the Truth.
If you have mistakenly taken money
to be the goal and not the means,
then money won't serve you.

14

The Money Mantra

Money is God's creativity
with which man keeps playing
the game of illusion.

There are many characteristics of money that are typical, one of which is that money can be saved.

While buying anything, those who are wise do not like to give away extra money unnecessarily. Not only do they bargain and save money, but also know how to invest that saved money. Anyone can save small amounts of money by bargaining, but the real skill lies in safely investing it for growth. Real saving is not just about saving, but also investing and multiplying your savings.

Someone who had quit his habit of smoking used to brag, "by quitting the habit of smoking, I have saved at least Rs. 500 every month." When he was asked, "So, where are the 500 rupees that you saved every month?" he was tongue-tied. He had no answer because he didn't know where the Rs. 500 was spent. He did save money but did not save his savings; he spent them all!

To become money-wise, you need to change your spending habit. If you are able to save on cash expenses, you should keep the saved cash away from the wallet. Do not spend it. Stash it away in a piggy bank and later (once the piggy bank fills up) transfer it in your bank account.

Using the money mantra – Touch money with the feeling of abundance

Whenever you are about to give money to others, take a moment to feel the touch of the money; feel its vibration. Whatever kind of money you are holding in your hand, i.e., notes, coins, cards, cheque, or even your abstract bank balance, just as you are about to give (or transfer) it, focus your attention on it for a moment and tell yourself, "This money is going to return to me manifold… There is enough!" This is the money mantra. Just shift your attention to the 'touch' between the currency and your hand while giving money. If you are transferring funds online, visualize the worth of that amount. Do not bring any emotional attachment to it. This touch or visualization will give you a different feeling. You may not have done this earlier, but try it now, and experience the multifold return of money.

To summarize, whenever you are about to give money or transfer funds, focus on the money, touch it, visualize it, and repeat the money mantra. You can follow these steps even while depositing money in your bank or savings box. This habit will enhance your understanding and awareness of money. Your savings will begin to multiply.

The Miracle of Saving

> A man used to buy peanuts from a street-vendor every day. While eating peanuts, he would always complain to the vendor, "I have a money problem. Money never stays with me." One day, the vendor gave him a bag full of peanuts. The man exclaimed, "What are you doing?! I don't need so many peanuts." The vendor replied, "This is *your* bag." On hearing this, the man said, "Are you

crazy? I buy peanuts worth one rupee only, not a bagful." The peanut-vendor then explained, "Sir, this is your bag. Every time you bought peanuts worth a rupee, I kept a few peanuts aside from those, which you never noticed. Those one or two peanuts every day have now added up to this bagful of peanuts."

The man was pleasantly shocked, 'Wow! Even one or two peanuts a day can create such wonders!' He then realized that there was a lot of money that was coming in his life, but he had underestimated the power of small savings.

Thus, 80% of the money problems can be resolved with the habit of saving and spending wisely. Howsoever poor one may be, one can still inculcate the habit of saving. **Little drops of water make a lake; therefore, don't underestimate the power of small savings.**

Plan in such a way that your money fetches you more money. Even the greatest of treasures will eventually run dry if you just keep spending. If you can save even a few coins daily, this saving could later add up to a great fortune. It is important to understand the difference between being a miser and being a wise saver, and imbibe the good habit of saving money.

Exercise-

Contemplate on the various everyday situations where you can save little peanuts (money). For example, money saved by selling scrap lying in the house. Keep this money in your piggy bank, and once it is full, you deposit it in your bank account and invest it in mutual funds or create a recurring deposit.

Let Money Beget More Money

Man usually keeps worrying about what is not there.
Seldom does he talk about what is there.
Such negative thinking drains away his wealth.

If making money is the first step, and saving money the second step, then multiplying money is the next important step. If you have reached this step, then it is necessary to understand a few facts.

Every month saving one out of ten parts of your wealth will go a big way. Apart from using this tenth part for enhancing your skills, you can also set aside some part of it to multiply it in consultation with an expert. Invest it in the right undertakings so that it keeps growing. Stagnant water stinks while flowing water remains sparkling clean, and fresh. In the same way, hoarded money gets polluted (blocked). Hence it is essential to let money grow by investing it in the right avenues.

Investing money with the help of expert advice can reap good results. Get advice from people who have learned the right way to multiply money through their own experience and mistakes. Use their advice to make more money from the money you already have.

Learn to make your money work for you. Your money should be placed in the right endeavors to let it grow.

Many people get entangled in fraudulent schemes in the hope of becoming rich and lose all their hard-earned money quickly. This leads to life-long repentance. We should beware of such frauds, and not fall prey to hollow promises of becoming millionaires overnight. The propagators of such fraud schemes can misguide us with promises of higher returns in the shorter term. Such apparently lucrative but dubious promises do nothing but complicate life.

Once we follow the guidelines provided by established experts with discretion, we will see that the tree of prosperity continues to grow, our potential savings increase and our principal amount fetches good interest. We should not give in to the temptation of spending the interest amount, else our money tree will never flourish.

When we refrain from spending the interest, we can take advantage of the power of compounding by letting the interest amount fetch further interest. Savings lead to even more savings. By spending away the interest in a jiffy, we would damage our money tree. If we follow this rule with consistency and faith, then all our money-related problems can disappear. On learning this secret of abundance, we can find opportunities that will bring us good fortune.

Many people get caught up in the cycle of fate and say, "If we are destined to attain wealth, then it will come to us. Else it will not." We do not have to fall into the trap of fate since Lady Luck never favors anyone continuously. What have people, who won a fortune, or a lottery, or a bet at the racecourse, achieve? Soon, they go back to square one, where they are penniless. Hence, there is no sense in running behind fortune-tellers and following their predictions.

People don't give importance to the knowledge of prosperity.

Suppose there are two boxes placed in front of you. One box contains one lakh rupees, and the other contains a book that explains how money can grow in your life and how it should be used. If you were given a choice, which box would you choose?

Most people tend to choose the box containing one lakh rupees. And within no time, they would be back in the same financial position as they were earlier because they do not know how to use money in the right manner. Instead of giving importance to the knowledge of prosperity, most people value temporary happiness or pleasure that vanishes away in a short time. Very few would give importance to the knowledge of prosperity that is given in the book. After gaining this knowledge, the tree of prosperity begins to grow in life.

We should not delay gaining the right understanding about money. This understanding will help us in making the right choices for investing it. We will see that we not only achieve growth of money, but also attain peace, fulfillment, and lasting happiness in our life. By attaining happiness, there won't be any need to be jealous towards the rich, since we would know the principle of attracting abundance in our life through happiness.

If you want to earn money,
stop running away from hard work.
Awaken to the understanding of abundance.

16

Don't Envy the Rich

If you want to attain prosperity,
you should not harbor hatred
for prosperous people.

In money matters, man often makes the mistake of being envious and jealous of rich people. If one wants to be rich, but hates rich people, then how can he become rich? To welcome abundance in life, envy and malice need to be eliminated by attaining wisdom and inspiration. Prosperity comes when one is open and receptive to abundance. By harboring hatred or envy for wealthy people, they unknowingly block the flow of wealth in their lives.

It is good to appreciate others' success. Be happy when a neighbor or colleague wins a lottery and congratulate him. The reason to be happy is that if your neighbor has won a lottery, then you too can win one. If someone is getting rich in your neighborhood, then tomorrow, you too stand a chance of becoming affluent. Instead of lamenting, "My neighbor has this thing, but I don't," you can draw inspiration from him. Harboring jealousy or loathing creates money blocks.

Respecting Money

During the festival of Diwali, people worship Goddess Lakshmi—the Goddess of Wealth. This signifies respect and receptivity for wealth. Respect for money is an indication that you want prosperity in your life. By considering money as pieces of paper and stuffing it carelessly, amounts to disrespecting money. If you keep your money with care in your purse, it shows that you are respecting it. In this way, your vibration starts resonating with that of money. You get attuned to it. Whatever you are attuned to, easily comes in your life.

Suppose you are traveling by bus. You buy the ticket. The bus conductor tells you that he does not have the change for Rs. 10 and that he will give it to you later. But he doesn't. You think, 'It's ok, after all, it's just a matter of 10 rupees. If he doesn't return it, it won't make any difference to my wealth.' Though it may not seem that way, this act of yours indicates that you are disrespecting money. Although ten rupees may be a very small amount for you, but it's *your* money. And you should ask for it from the conductor; don't shy away from asking. You may give those ten rupees to needy people; but do collect it from the conductor. This, in principle, will mean that you respect money and are not irresponsible about it.

Many people believe that it does not make any difference to them if they don't get back their change. However, this is not true. It is fine if the other person is unable to return our change, but we need to at least make an effort to ask for it. This does not mean we have to fight for it, but we can surely ask for it politely. It is fine if he hasn't got the change. The point is that we should expect even ten rupees back without ignoring it.

This is respect for money. If we respect money, money will respect us. Many people squander their money by giving it to others indiscriminately. We don't have to get into any such extremes—neither throw it nor hoard it. We have to use it the right way, with understanding.

Be happy on seeing others prosper.
You will then become receptive to prosperity.

17

Use Money to Boost Health and Happiness

*Those who have some talent or art
do not need to worry about money.
Hence invest money in learning
and achieving competence in some skill or art.*

'Money' is not bad by itself, but it can be detrimental if it is associated with evils. Water poured in a vessel takes the shape of that vessel; in a glass, it takes the shape of the glass; in a pot, it takes the shape of the pot. Similarly, all the money present in this world is a pure entity, which changes its nature according to the whims and desires of the person possessing it. If you utilize money to walk the path of Truth and aren't egoistic about your wealth, then it can be said that money is being rightly used in your life. Else some people become arrogant on acquiring money.

Money is a neutral object; hence there is no need to be egoistic or pompous about it. As you are, so is your money. Money shapes itself as per the nature of the person possessing it. With an evil person, it helps in his evil activities. With a virtuous person, it helps in his benevolent activities. If you have the right understanding, then money becomes a boon; else it's a bane.

When money is given to a sorrowful person, it will augment his sorrow. When a person is sad, he lacks understanding, which is why his level of consciousness drops. When an arrogant person is given money, he becomes more arrogant. He keeps thinking, "I'll set this person right…" Hence, unknowingly, an arrogant person keeps multiplying his sorrows. A criminal will commit more crimes on getting money; he will trouble people all the more. Money makes him feel excited and powerful from within; so, he beats people and even resorts to killing them.

> One day a man won a lottery and was walking down the road proudly. On the way, one of his friends saw him and said, "Wow! Today you are looking very happy; what's the matter?" On hearing this, he gave his friend a tight slap. The friend was taken aback. He couldn't bear this insult, so he complained to the village chief, "For no fault of mine, this man slapped me."
>
> The chief decided to take action, called the man and asked him, "Did you slap your friend?" He arrogantly said, "Yes, I did." The chief asked him to pay a penalty of Rs. 500 to his friend for his offense. He agreed to pay the penalty. He put his hand in his pocket, gave one more slap to his friend, and then handed him a thousand rupee note. When he was questioned about his shocking behavior, he replied, "I didn't have any change. I had a thousand rupee note. Since the penalty for one slap is Rs. 500, it would be Rs. 1000 for two slaps. So, I slapped him once again and gave him Rs. 1000. The account is settled."

This may sound like an impractical joke. But it shows how man is unaware that his mind is taking him astray and wasting his energy in wrong activities. He is no longer worried about his friends or relatives anymore. In this way, instead of being a blessing, money turns into a curse by aggravating his ego. He is not aware that he is sowing the seeds of misery for the future through his actions.

On the other hand, when money is given to a truly happy person, he will spread more happiness around. Hence, first, be truly happy, attain the eternal bliss which is present within you. You will then utilize money for your happiness and health, and also that of others.

In the rat race to earn more and more money, people first spoil their health and then spend this hard-earned money to regain their lost health. Initially they work, day in and day out, put their body and mind through a lot of trouble, and thus invite diseases. They lose their health to attain wealth. Now to get their health back, they have to run behind doctors and pay them their hard-earned money.

This is how rich, ignorant people lead their life. Doctors may warn them not to eat sweets, stay away from excess fats and high-calorie food, be careful about salt intake, etc. But without paying any heed to the doctor's advice, they indulge in fulfilling their taste buds and ego. Thus, the irony is while a person was earning for his stomach (bread and butter), later his health deteriorates to the extent that he cannot put anything in his stomach, although he has got all the luxuries of the world. Hence, one needs to raise one's awareness and put a stop to the meaningless race behind money.

Looking at others chasing money, do not get diverted from your aim. Instead, give a better meaning to life by investing in health and happiness. Focus on the ultimate aim of this life and attain the ultimate truth.

To earn wealth, people destroy their health.
Then to earn their health,
people destroy (spend) their wealth.

18

Stop the Meaningless Rat-race for Money

When the Goddess of Wealth is pleased with us,
we are not constantly reminded of money.
The Goddess is displeased with those who always
think about money, even if they are millionaires.

The first person who started the race for 'only money' left this world long ago. But now, most people are in the rush for acquiring and preserving wealth. They have forgotten the real understanding of money. Seeing other people running after money, they emulate them.

What happens with people who run behind money and finally get it? Suddenly they feel aimless. In this state, they make even bigger financial goals. In this way, they join the blind race of making money their endless goal.

To acquire money is not bad, but it is wrong to forget the real purpose behind money. Awaken your awareness about money and decide what you are going to achieve with it. If you are clear about this, then money would not take you away from the ultimate aim of your life. Instead, it will help you reach the ultimate goal of Self-realization, for which you have attained human birth. It will guide you to take the right path of spirituality in your life.

Do not compare or make assumptions

We've already discussed that people lead a miserable life only because of their habit of comparison. "My neighbor is doing this, so I too need to do this." Thousands of people buy cars; one may not have any problem with that. Thousands of people build luxurious mansions; but it may not be a concern. But as soon as one's neighbor buys a car, one starts feeling miserable. As soon as one's neighbor builds a huge mansion, one feels distraught. This is the cause of unhappiness. This is how man thinks. With his limited intelligence, man thinks that everybody, except his neighbor, should progress. All his comparison is with his neighbor. As long as his neighbor does not move ahead of him, he has no problem.

Seeing others' cars and mansions, we assume that these people are very happy because they have all the luxuries of life. On seeing a person pass by in a swanky car, we assume that he must be very happy. We equate happiness with the car. "Only when I own a luxurious car, will I be happy." Whenever we see anything, we feel, "I too need this." But do we give a moment to consider what's exactly going on in the mind of the car's owner? He could perhaps be in a depressed state of mind. But we do not see that just because of his swanky car. Therefore, we shouldn't make assumptions or judge people based on their external appearances. Appearances can be deceptive. The external appearance need not reveal the person's mental state. Seeing people doing something, we too feel that we should be doing that, which may not be necessary or important. Hence, we need to be aware while making such decisions by comparing ourselves with others.

The Goddess of Wealth demands proof

The Goddess of Wealth is pleased with those who are cautious. She eludes those who are careless. She expects evidence from people to understand whether they can take care of money or not. She blesses those who can provide her with such evidence. If we can safeguard money and let it grow, she feels confident that we can handle more money.

Usually, people fall into two extremes: misers who hoard money, making money their master, and squanderers who waste money in futile pursuits. Without getting into these extremes, treat the money you possess as nature's wealth kept in your custody. Save and invest it appropriately so that it keeps growing. If you have understood this fact, then the Goddess of Wealth will be pleased with you. Do not waste your hard-earned money to feign false grandeur. Pay attention to its safety and growth.

When the Goddess of Wealth is pleased with you, you do not keep thinking about money. She eludes those who constantly think about and hanker after her, some despite being billionaires. Those with whom the Goddess of Wealth is pleased are blessed with money at the right time whenever they face financial constraints. Therefore, offer the right prayer to the Goddess of Wealth with devotion and always entertain godly thoughts. There is no scarcity of anything in godly thoughts. There is abundance of time, love, happiness, health, wealth, and contentment.

Pray to the Goddess of Wealth

The wheel of worldly attractions (*Maya*) is continuously on the move. If you wish to break free off this illusory cycle, then it will help to pray to Maya: "Bestow your grace upon us; please set me free from your web of illusion."

While worshipping the Goddess of Wealth, pray for liberation from the illusory web of her charm. Pray with utmost faith, feeling, and fervor. If you genuinely wish to free yourself from the clutches of Maya, then the Goddess of Wealth will be pleased with you and release you from this never-ending cycle. If the Goddess of Wealth is pleased, then it would not take much time for the Goddess' consort - Satyanarayana (the Supreme Truth) to appear in your life. With the awakening of the Supreme Truth, you will attain the real goal of human birth.

Let us learn the right way of praying to the Goddess of Wealth, Goddess of Prosperity (Lakshmi) and get a glimpse of the Truth (God, Self) residing within us. Only then will our inner lamp be ignited, the flame of this lamp being the Consciousness due to which we are alive.

> O Goddess of Prosperity!
> I am your devotee; I wish to please you.
> When you are pleased with us,
> we are not reminded of you.
> When you are displeased with us,
> we cannot stop thinking about you.
> The ones with whom you are happy,
> do not think about you all day.
> The ones with whom you are unhappy,
> are always stressed about money.
> Please do come to us
> even before we are reminded of you.
> Please bring Narayana (wisdom) along
> whenever you come.
> You are our well-wishing mother.
> You know very well what is good for your children.
> Hence, please grant us the boon
> that the ego within us should not grow
> with your arrival in our life.
> O Goddess, please accept our prayer!

19

Consciously Sow the Seeds of Faith

*When one becomes indolent after acquiring
all conveniences that money can buy,
then money becomes a curse.*

We've heard or seen people worshipping and offering prayers at temples situated at mountaintops or on the banks of rivers. They feel that if they offer prayer in a particular temple, their wishes will be fulfilled. They have tremendous faith, and with that power of faith, their wishes do get fulfilled. People lay down these wishes through various rituals, donations, or fasting – these methods act as seeds of faith. These seeds of faith reap miracles in their lives.

As we sow, so shall we reap. If we plant a seed of lemon, we will get a lemon tree. So, if we sow a seed of faith for a particular wish, we reap the fulfillment of that wish.

Those who can consciously sow the seed of faith have their wishes fulfilled. But if they sow their seeds in ignorance or with blind faith, they may not receive what they really wish. By sowing the wrong seeds, man continues to live in the cycle of joy and sorrow. If we sow the seed of faith with awareness, we experience a miracle that is necessary for us today. A miracle that can pull us out of our financial constraints. But for that miracle, we need to sow the seed of faith today. The seed of faith is nature's system and method of working. This method lifts us above all our difficulties and gives us whatever we wish for.

Law of Faith

The emphasis on faith is because it is the most powerful factor in your financial success. Whatever you believe intensely becomes your reality.

A successful person has total faith in his ability to succeed. He doesn't even think, talk, or worry about the possibilities of failure. This faith becomes the cause of his success. Thoughts of failure do not trouble him; hence negative thoughts do not obstruct his work.

You need to work patiently on developing your faith. To accomplish your financial goals, you need to keep complete faith that you are going to achieve your goal. This faith is an important step that helps you in achieving your goal. And if this faith is accompanied by a positive attitude, then it works wonders. Positive attitude helps and augments the belief that – *come what may; I will succeed*. That is how the law of faith works. Hence, if you have the faith that you will succeed, you also need to learn the art of sowing the right seeds of faith.

To sow the seeds of faith, first assess your life to identify the seeds you have sown in the past and what have you reaped from them. *You will reap what you have sown*. This is the irrefutable law of nature. You have achieved according to what you have sown in your personal and professional life. If you put in hard work, abidance of rules, discipline, and self-confidence, you will certainly get respect, love, harmony, and prosperity. You shall reap the fruits as per the seeds you have sown. Nature is preset to her rules. You cannot manipulate or deceive these rules.

If you rewind and reflect on every aspect of your life's story: your surroundings, your health, wealth, relationships, method of working, happiness of your near and dear ones, professional security, etc., you will notice that you have got everything as per what you had sown. You are reaping the fruits of the seeds you have sown in the past.

If, for some reason, you are not happy with the way things are happening at present, then change the seeds that you are sowing today. If you were sowing the seeds of negativity and glum, it's time to shift to the seeds of positivity and optimism. If you want something different or special in your life, you need to sow something different or special. Just as a farmer who sows various types of seeds to reap an abundance of various types of crops, you too need to sow different thoughts and actions to get the best and extraordinary results.

The Magic Box

By now, you must be habituated to writing your budget in a diary, laptop, or your mobile phone. This would be ensuring that all your financial requirements are being fulfilled. Nevertheless, there would be times when certain wishes remain unfulfilled despite budgeting for them. Here's a little trick that can help you realize some of your unfulfilled wishes.

For such desires, you can create a magic box. A magic box is a simple box made with wood or cardboard just as you would have a piggy bank. Stick a label on the magic box that says: 'I expect miracles daily!' Write down your unfulfilled desires on pieces of paper and drop it in this box with full faith. Write your unfulfilled desires in a positive or affirmative tone. If you want to buy a car and it seems as if it's not happening soon, you can create a note: "According to my Divine plan, I now own my dream car." While you create this note, fill yourself with the feeling of positivity and faith that nature will answer your prayer. Feel that the miracle is already happening. With this faith, drop the note in the magic box. Your faith will help in manifesting your dreams faster.

To get the best, give the best to the best

A farmer never keeps aside bad grains for sowing in the next season. He preserves the best part of the present crop for sowing. He does this to reap a better, nutritious, and abundant harvest the next time.

The farmer opts for the best. He knows nature's secret: To get the best, give the best to the best. But a common man does not follow this in his life.

You need to ask yourself, "What is the best that I have given?" When you visited the temple or the church, what was the best that you gave? Did you offer flowers and prayers with love and devotion? Did you promise to give up any of your unwanted habits? Did you make a vow? Or did you just go for leisure? What are you offering to nature (God) from what you have? It is only when you give something or sow a seed that God works to multiply it. This is as if God is telling you, "Give me the seed of faith, devotion, purity, unconditional love first, so that I can begin to work on multiplying it."

You expect success, comforts, good health, security, love, confidence, fame, money, and so forth from God. But in turn, what are you first giving to God to work upon?

You have seen how a seed sown in the soil grows and multiplies into a bumper harvest. Everyone is left spellbound beholding this miracle. Everybody feels overjoyed by seeing this gift of nature. This miracle takes place by sowing the best seeds in the best land, at the best time.

Once the farmer sows the seeds, he does not leave his farm until the harvest season. He takes care of the farm and waits patiently. We, too, need to be like the farmer. We need to sow our seeds of faith, without leaving our field. The seed of faith could mean any of the following or similar:

- Donating money for some noble cause
- Helping somebody
- Listening compassionately to somebody's sorrow
- Happily giving someone your time
- Praying sincerely for others
- Serving someone who is in need

- Teaching an illiterate to read and write
- Becoming a medium for someone's growth and development
- Helping someone monetarily
- Solving someone's difficulties using your skill, understanding, and wisdom
- Feeding the hungry
- Arranging medicines for the sick
- Helping someone to get rid of ignorance

On sowing our seed of faith, we shouldn't lose our patience and run away from our problems. We should keep faith that if we have sown the seed of faith, it will surely yield results. We need to persevere and stay put to reap the fruit. If we get scared of testing situations or leave the ground in dejection, it would mean that we have lost faith in God's benevolent providence.

Man leaves his ground of action because he faces difficulties in life, due to which his faith begins to falter. Some difficulties arise due to colleagues or neighbors, some may be due to one's boss at the workplace or spouse at home, some could be due to the weather, health, the news, etc. Whatever be the source of these troubles, one needs to understand that these troubles have come to teach them the lessons of life.

If we have sown the seed of faith, we need to wait patiently, having full conviction that our difficulty will be resolved miraculously due to the seed of faith that we have sown. God works on the seed of faith we have sown, and returns it to us, multiplying it a thousand times in the form of wealth, health, love, skills, and fulfillment. We need to wait for a little while with faith. We shouldn't cause any trouble to God by leaving our field of action, nor should we make Him run after us to give us our fruit! It would be like someone depositing a cheque in a bank to withdraw cash and not waiting to collect it.

The importance of consciously sowing the seed of faith

Until now, you have done a lot; you have given a lot to God too. In other words, you have sown several seeds of faith. But it is possible that these seeds may have been sown unconsciously. You may have expected something from certain people in return, instead of expecting from God. This ignorance, lack of faith and awareness becomes the reason for suffering. Sow your seeds of faith, i.e., help the creations of God with the genuine intention, "I am offering this help to God as a seed of faith" and expect only from God. In return, God will fulfill all your necessities.

We have forgotten the power of *giving*. We believe that by giving, we will be at loss. But the fact is that whatever we give to others returns manifold. Happiness increases several times by sharing and reduces by holding back. Therefore, we should learn to give.

In this world, there is nobody who has nothing to give to others. You can remove the thorns present in someone's way, wipe someone's tears, or bring a smile on the face of a sad person. You can pray for someone, give your time, information, or knowledge to someone who needs it. It does not matter what you give or how much you give. What's important is 'giving'. He, who gives, receives a lot, and when he receives a lot, he gives even more. This is how this virtuous cycle of giving perpetuates itself.

Charity or donation also amounts to sowing the seeds of faith that yield a good harvest. God needs the seeds of faith to work upon, but without sowing any seeds, many people only keep praying and then they complain that their prayers are not being answered. Thus, they first need to understand God's method of working.

Giving money, time, or helping someone unconditionally can also act as the seed of faith. You can expect miracles by sowing these seeds of faith.

As important as the act of donation is, equally important it is to understand the beneficiary's eligibility. If money is donated by keeping this aspect in mind, it yields the best fruit – in fact, the supreme fruit of eternal bliss.

Think over as to whom you should donate money:

1. If you donate money to an assassin, he may buy weapons of violence.
2. If you donate money to a drunkard, he will drink liquor with it.
3. If you donate money to a sick person, he will buy medicines with it.
4. If you donate money to a Truth seeker, he will set out on the path of seeking the Truth.
5. If you donate money to one who renders selfless service, he will increase his acts of service.

Hence while donating money, keep in mind, and implement the following do's and don'ts:

1. Donate from a part of your necessities.
2. Donate with understanding; be instrumental for others' growth.
3. Ascertain whether the beneficiary deserves the charity.
4. Donate according to the recipient's need.
5. Always be careful so as not to pass on the feeling of inferiority to the beneficiary.
6. Donate with an open mind and the pure joy of giving.
7. Do not donate with an intention for fame or any kind of appreciation or returns.
8. Charity should not be a matter of business; it should be unconditional.
9. The feeling of ownership and ego (my wealth, my house, my children) should disappear with charity. It should teach us the art of living in harmony with the feeling of oneness. We should attain liberation from the attractions of the material world.

10. It would be the best to donate to make someone self-reliant.

11. Thank the person to whom you are donating for the opportunity to give. This will ensure that your ego does not bloat.

12. Do not consider a small donation as meager.

> One day, on the occasion of a festival, an announcement was made in a village to make donations to the church. All the villagers gathered in the church and started offering their donations one by one. Jesus was also present there. At the end of the day, Jesus proclaimed, "The greatest donation of the day has come from an old lady." People were surprised. They brought forth the lady. On being asked how much she had donated, she said she had donated a quarter. Hearing this, all the wealthy people were furious and asked, "We have donated such huge amounts, then how can her meager donation be considered the biggest?!"
>
> Jesus explained, "Those, who donated thousands, have millions. From those millions, if a few thousands are removed, it may not make much of a difference to them. On the contrary, this old lady had just a quarter, and she really needed it. But she chose to forsake her need and donated it. Hence this donation is the biggest donation today."
>
> All the villagers hung their heads down in shame. They understood that compared to the huge donations made by the rich, the meager donations made by the poor are more important. This is because these small amounts are also a big sacrifice for the poor.

We need to be clear about what we want in life. Do we want wisdom, self-confidence, and Self Realization? Or do we wish for comforts, luxuries, profits, security, and riches? We need to decide on this first and then pray to God, "Now I shall be giving my best to You (love, money, energy, attention, knowledge, time, etc.) and shall then expect the best from You." We don't have to beg anything from God. God Himself does not wish to see anyone begging from Him.

As per His rules, God wishes to give man everything in abundance. He makes us know these rules through nature. In nature, one single seed produces innumerable seeds. A seed of weeds (seed of distrust) gives rise to a harvest of weeds (sorrows). A seed of fruit and flower (seed of faith) generates an abundant harvest of wholesome seeds (joys). Similarly, our good deeds, like those listed earlier, act as our seeds of faith. These seeds can create miracles in our life. To attain prosperity, we should start using this principle of nature right from today.

The feeling of generosity and our actions

There are two kinds of people in this world. The first ones allow their wealth to pile up and bring themselves a false sense of security. The second ones are those who use their prosperity to increase not only the happiness in their lives but also in the lives of others by being generous. We are truly successful if we can change the lives of others by being generous with our abundance. So, how do we become generous? How can our generosity show in our actions?

Firstly, we need to stop thinking that money will bring us security. It won't. It might make us feel more secure, and it might enable us to buy things right now, but money can vanish quite easily. We all have seen businesses going bankrupt and fortunes being lost. History is replete with the riches-to-rags stories of people who were once rich and lost everything one day. The biggest misunderstanding we have about money is that we need to accumulate as much as we can and preserve it. Hence, when we learn to give money, it not only affects us emotionally, but we also start breaking out of our insecurity.

Secondly, we need to focus on the happiness that others feel due to our generous acts. There are many people and institutions in this world that could gain from our acts of benevolence. They can use this help for the welfare of others. As a result, many needy people can receive help. A small gift from us can also be of big help to the needy in hard times, who will be delighted by it. Perhaps today, we may find it difficult to donate an amount of Rs. 3000, but we can certainly donate Rs—250 per month for a year.

We need to also make use of common sense while being generous. If we use our funds smartly, we will never get caught in financial problems owing to our generosity. By sponsoring a lunch, our bank balance won't run out. We can do something good for our relatives and friends; thereby, we will find love and warmth in our relationships.

Those who are philanthropists and help others, always receive all that they need. One of the very famous principles of John Wesley is: "Earn all you can, give all you can, save all you can." This principle brings money into the right situation. This is the key of successful people. Why do successful people in our field of activity have a higher income? What is different in whatever they do that others don't? We should emulate their wisdom every day with common sense.

There should be respect, not obsession, for money
There should be love, not attachment, for money
There should be understanding, not ignorance, about money
There should be contemplation, not worry, about money.

20

Time is Also Money

Give a proper position to money in your life
– neither too high nor too low.
Money is money; use it.
And forget it till the next need arises.
Earn money and use it as a means to an end.

Iron expands on heating. Whenever metal is heated, it changes its shape. Just as metal behaves according to its properties, prosperity too works according to certain principles. Let us understand one of these principles in this chapter.

Principle of Time

You can do just two things with your time—either spend it, or invest it.

When we invest money, we can get more in return. But when we spend time, it does not return. Money that is spent can be earned back. But that's not the case with time. Once gone, it's gone forever.

Entrepreneurs understand this principle and hence value their time. They use this priceless asset of time with a lot of awareness. We all are gifted with the same amount of time—the same number of hours, minutes each day. There is no bias in a way that someone has more time because he is an entrepreneur, and someone else has less time because he isn't. The difference lies in the importance and understanding that one gives to this precious asset.

Many people, who wish to prosper are found wasting their time in low-value work. This behavior tends to push them into the valley of hopelessness and failure. In other words, such people never succeed in achieving their goals.

One needs to be aware of the precious time they have. They need to continually introspect, "Whatever time I invest in this work, will it help me achieve my goal or will it mislead me?"

Let us perform a small exercise. Decide your annual financial target. Now divide the target by the total number of weeks you work. A person earning Rs. 2 lakhs annually, earns about Rs. 4000 per week. So, how much does he make per hour of his working day? Dividing the weekly earnings by the total number of working hours in a week will give you the value of one hour. A person who works 8 hours a day, works for 40 hours a week, so the value of his one work hour would be about Rs. 100.

Based on the total number of hours you want to work in a day, you can calculate the monetary value of one hour of work. You can decide: where you are today and where you want to go. With this simple calculation, you can decide your financial target and work towards achieving it.

How you manage your time helps in directing your efforts towards success. Your work then takes you from your current position to the point of success.

This exercise will help you find the value of one working hour. From today onwards, do ask yourself, "Will I be able to get the value of Rs. X from the work that I am doing now or planning to do? Will an hour of this work be able to provide me the value of Rs. X? Or should I invest my time in doing something better?"

If your answer is 'no', then you need not involve yourself in the work that will fetch you the desired returns. This does not mean that you should leave your job or not do that work. You should think about investing your time creatively such that it will help you go one step closer to your goal. You need not do that during your working hours. You can easily manage your social, family, and self-development activities in your remaining time, such as listening to discourses, reading good books, rendering service, working on upgrading your skills, etc. Balancing your time in this way will help you achieve your life's chosen goal.

By learning this skill of time management, you can now think about how you can complete your tasks effectively, in the right manner, and with the right priority. You have to find a middle path to complete the task without wasting your time. In this way, derive full advantage of this rule of time management.

The Laws of Nature

A miser never works to develop his capabilities.
He relies on lady luck and is caught up in the wheel of fortune.
Hence, he doesn't develop the ability to earn.

There was a couple who lived an ordinary life. They used to donate some money every month. Under no circumstances could they afford to donate millions of rupees. But they had a definite aim in mind: "Before our last breath, we should be capable enough to donate millions." They had complete faith in accomplishing their aim. This is because they were pursuing their aim properly and systematically.

The only thought in their mind was: "Towards the end of our lives, when we look back at our generosity, we should find that we did something worthwhile." You, too, can become successful in achieving your aim if you work systematically with a plan and remain firm in implementing your plans.

In this chapter here, we shall read about some important Laws of Nature that can help us grow not just financially but on other facets of life too.

Law of cause and effect

This is such a profound and powerful law that it is termed by many as the 'iron law' of destiny. Whatever happens in life, happens according to this law.

In simple words, it means that whatever effects you see in your life always have a preceding cause or causes to it. The bottom line is that if you want to achieve anything in your life or if you harbor a burning desire for something, and you have marked it, then you will achieve it. For this, you need to find the causes that lead you to that effect, and then implement those causes (perform those actions) in your life.

Financial success is an effect; there are particular causes behind it. If any one person can do some work and attain wealth, then you, too, can do that work and attain wealth. Similarly, if you implement those causes in some other field, you will get the same results that others have. This is not a miracle; neither is this law dependent on fate.

If you want to be a successful and prosperous person in your chosen profession, you need to follow the mental footsteps of those who have achieved the peak of wealth and success in your profession. By repeating what they have done, and perhaps improving upon it, eventually, you would get the desired results.

Law of Concentration

Whatever you focus on get attracted in your life and start growing. When you constantly think about your aim and the things you desire, those thoughts become powerful and magnetic. These thoughts then attract and manifest your desire.

If you want to become a successful businessman, you should actually see yourself doing those things that will make your wish come true. If you focus on your desire with complete concentration, it will manifest faster in your life. On the contrary, if you think on those things you are afraid of or on those things you don't want, your fear will aggravate. This fear will dominate your thoughts and make you commit errors. Inadvertently, you harm yourself by thinking about things you don't want.

Quite often, we tend to avoid those very things we should be doing to achieve our aim. On the other hand, we can more easily do all those things that drive us away from our aim, because such things do not require much hard work. The fact is that the more negative we think, the more these thoughts affect our life.

This law of concentration can be considered the sub-law of the law of cause and effect. Only those people who consistently focus on their aim attain success. People who contemplate on the things that they **do not** want in their lives are the ones who fail. Consequently, successful people become more successful, while those who fail, encounter even more failures.

You need to consistently focus on and visualize how you want to see yourself in the future, the wealth you want to earn. From dawn to dusk, you should do those activities that will maintain your speed towards making you a successful person. Make a firm resolution to keep your words and actions away from those things that divert you from your aim. And make sure that you abide by your resolution.

Law of Attraction

According to the law of attraction, you are a magnet, and your thoughts and feelings create a magnetic field around you. Any thought you entertain is associated with a positive or negative feeling and is released from your mind. It then attracts people, events, ideas, and opportunities in your life that are consistent with it.

According to this principle, if you have a clear picture of achieving your goal (or you have a desire to become rich) and hold that picture constantly in your mind, you will definitely attract whatever you want to achieve. All those people who have been successful or prosperous have held the image of their aim firmly and constantly in their mind until they realized it.

Law of Correspondence

The law of correspondence is a powerful principle. According to this law, your external world is but a mirror of your inner world. Whatever happens within you (in your subconscious mind) is what manifests outside. According to this law, whatever event is taking place outside is a reflection of what is happening within you.

'Your outer world is a reflection of your inner world.' This means that if you can firmly hold your aim with total awareness in your conscious and subconscious mind for a prolonged duration, you gradually see it manifest in the outer world.

This law applies to the financial facet of your life too. Hence, consciously focus your thoughts on your financial aspirations. Gradually these will manifest in reality in your outer world, and you will achieve your aim.

Attain Real Wealth

What can money not buy?
Money cannot buy inner silence,
nor can it buy true love or true happiness.

There was a man named Mr. Prosperity. Every day, he would pray to God, "O God, please bless me with prosperity so that I can attain fulfillment."

One night, he received a message in his dream, which said: "Tomorrow, you will meet three people. Ask them to give their wealth to you. By doing so, your prayers will be answered."

Mr. Prosperity was overjoyed that God had appeared in his dream and showed him the way to his fulfillment. He set out the next morning, and indeed, as prophesied in his dream, he met three people one after the other on the way.

The first one he came across was a wealthy man. He approached the wealthy man, and based on the instruction in his dream, he hesitantly said, "Please give me your wealth."

The rich man kicked him and screamed at him, "Get the hell out of here! How dare you ask for my wealth?!"

The second person Mr. Prosperity met, was a hermit. Fearfully, Mr. Prosperity asked him to give his wealth. Hearing this, the hermit handed over his empty bowl to him. Mr. Prosperity was taken aback, thinking about what the hermit was giving him. He immediately slipped out of there.

Further ahead, he met the third person, who looked quite ordinary. Mr. Prosperity approached him and narrated the whole story to him. The ordinary-looking man took out a diamond from his pocket and gave it to him, saying, "This is my entire wealth, take it."

Mr. Prosperity was elated. He started thinking that now all his problems and difficulties will come to an end. He will now attain every success and feel fulfilled.

Happily, he took the diamond and returned home. However, he could not sleep that night; he could not stop thinking. Early next morning, he went and stood on the same path where he had met the person who gave him the diamond. He waited for him the entire day, but that person was nowhere in sight. He tried the next day too but in vain. Eventually, after three days, he spotted that man.

Mr. Prosperity immediately went up to him and stopped him. With mixed feelings of joy and excitement, Mr. Prosperity asked him, "Why didn't you give me your real wealth? The rich man had kicked me off, the hermit scared me by handing me the begging bowl, and you got away very shrewdly."

The man was astonished. He said, "What's wrong? I gave you the wealth you had asked for; I gave you the diamond!" Mr. Prosperity replied, "Yes, you gave me this diamond, but this is not your real wealth. I haven't been able to sleep since that day. I kept thinking about how easily you gave away the diamond to me. What is that understanding, that knowledge you possess because of which you could so easily part with this invaluable diamond? I want that knowledge, on the basis of which you were able to take such a big step without any hesitation. That wisdom is your real wealth. On reaching home, I realized that I wouldn't get fulfillment from this diamond, but through the understanding that you possess."

The ordinary-looking man said, "You too have this real wealth; it is within you. You just need to seek that place within where the Universal Self associates with your body-mind. With the help of meditation, you need to dive in and learn the art of being there. Once you understand this, making decisions will be easy for you too. You will not face shortage of money, and nobody can steal this real wealth."

"Raise your awareness; elevate your level of consciousness, which is your greatest wealth. As long as you possess this wealth, there won't be any dearth of joy and satisfaction in your life. Always keep a watchful eye on this wealth of yours to ensure that it does not diminish. What you keep your eye on can never be stolen."

In the above story, the first rich person Mr. Prosperity came across was a worldly man; the second one was a hermit; and the third one was a Bright worldly person or *Tej Sansari*. 'Bright' or 'Tej' means the state beyond two polarities. Here Bright-worldly person signifies one who is beyond a worldly man as well as a recluse.

That day, Mr. Prosperity, who depicts a worldly man, realized that understanding, awareness, silence, meditation, time, and love are the most valuable treasures present within us.

You, too, can become truly rich by being a Bright worldly person. Do not accept any false beliefs about money; bring all your beliefs to light. Do not allow money to use you; but use money as a means to attain your ultimate goal of permanent happiness (the Supreme Truth that is present within you).

The next chapter elaborates the life of a Bright worldly person. it explains how such a life differs from one that is a recluse who has renounced the world, as well as one who is indulging in the world indiscriminately.

Neither be a Worldly Person, Nor a Recluse

For a worldly person,
failure is sorrow and misery.
For a Bright worldly person,
failure is a preparation for progress.

A common worldly man goes to school, earns his livelihood, gets married, gives birth to children, and raises them just as he had been. This holds true for every worldly man or householder. Education, occupation to earn money, marriage, children, and retirement—he turns this wheel his entire life.

But a *Tej Sansari*—a 'Bright' worldly man—has the supreme knowledge of Truth *(Tejgyan)*. Hence, he clearly understands the true meaning and significance of money, relationships, the Truth of life, and the purpose of his visit to earth.

A Bright worldly person understands the following four points very clearly:

1. Everything has been created in abundance for everyone, including money. Money, time, love and happiness are available in abundance for each one of us.

2. Money does not impede spiritual growth. In fact, through right use of money, we can enhance our own and others' spiritual development.

3. Money is a path, not the goal. And being a path, it has its own importance. Money is not a bad thing. Regarding money to be the goal, people have unconsciously caused hurdles in their lives. Many people hold beliefs such as: "We can consider that we have fulfilled our life's purpose if we earn this much money." With such thinking, people have placed limitations in their lives and their happiness.

4. How money is generated, how it flows, how it grows, when its flow stops in our lives, what are the impediments in the flow of money, and how to boost the flow of money.

Qualities of a Bright worldly person

A Bright worldly person is the only hope to bring about a transformation in this world. This is because such a person gives more importance to qualities rather than money. A Bright worldly person has the following attributes:

1. Unshakeable faith

The first and foremost quality of a Bright worldly person is unshakeable faith—faith that does not waver in any situation. This faith does not arise out of ignorance but from the understanding of the Truth. He views every event through the eyes of understanding and takes benefit of every event. He knows that Providence (God) that has given him life, will take care of him until his death. Hence, his prayers are imbued with the power of faith. This faith guides him every moment of his life. Even if he has to face sorrow in his life, his faith does not falter. Instead, he knows the secret behind sorrow and the lesson he has to learn from it.

2. Flexible Intellect

A Bright worldly person possesses the quality of flexibility. He can adapt himself to every person, place, and situation. He becomes a child with a child, mature with an elder person, and youthful with a youngster. A Bright worldly person's intellect is active and flexible. The trees which stand rigidly in storms get uprooted and destroyed, whereas the ones which bend with the winds are left unharmed. People lose love in their relationships because of their rigidity. Till the end of their lives, they never realize the virtue of unconditional, unlimited, true love.

3. Fearless Eyes

A Bright worldly person has fearless eyes. He is not scared of problems. Instead, problems shy away from him, leaving him with gifts (opportunities) that they bring along.

You, too, can become a Bright worldly person and become free from destiny and sorrow. One who **is free from fate is truly fortunate; one who is free from the doership of deeds is egoless, and the one who is free from freedom itself, is a Bright worldly person.**

A Bright worldly person: the world's paramount need

A Bright worldly person is one who is suitable for the world. He would not relinquish his worldly responsibilities and stay in the mountains or the jungles. Suppose a person, who is living in an ordinary house builds a bungalow but doesn't stay in it, what will you tell him? "Why did you build the bungalow if you wanted to stay in the ordinary house?" Similarly, this world has been created to stay and actively participate in it; not to escape from it. A Bright worldly person lives in this world (bungalow) and derives unconditional happiness, which is beyond joy and sorrow.

He is free from all limiting beliefs. By explaining the reason behind various false beliefs, he also frees his children from them. He knows the importance of harmony and understanding in relationships. The real purpose behind marriage is that two people come together and become instrumental in helping each other understand their true Self and attain Self Realization.

However, in today's world, this understanding does not exist. A lot many people are getting married and getting others married. People are tying the marital knot at a very young age. Thus, the ones who are fighting with each other like kids are giving birth and raising children. But the lack of understanding of a Bright worldly life, has dented these sacred relationships. For a Bright worldly person, **the meaning of relationships and life is not to slip and then try to regain balance; but to slip, gain balance, and get up—not empty-handed but picking up some lesson along the way.**

Every event in our life, be it a quarrel or a stressful situation or a happy incident, teaches us something and gives us some experience. We should benefit from it. If we do not learn from these experiences, these quarrels continue throughout our life.

The children who are brought up in this atmosphere grow up into sick adults. Here 'sick' means diseased with either inferiority or superiority complex. If such children are presented as citizens to our nation and our world; how will our nation's future be? And when these children grow up and bear their children, what would be the condition of our world? This is why the solution is to become a Bright worldly person by attaining the right understanding.

'Bright worldly life' is a new concept, a revolutionary idea. But it is the need of the world today. By adopting the best qualities of both—a worldly man and a recluse—a Bright worldly person knows his ultimate aim. Achieving this aim is his whole and sole intention. A Bright worldly person is out of the vicious circle of the worldly materialistic man and also far from being a recluse. So, let us now understand the demerits of a recluse and a worldly man.

Demerits of a recluse

The hermits who truly attained higher wisdom have almost disappeared. Most of those who appear to be hermits today are swindlers, who trap people in various rituals, thereby misleading them from their ultimate aim of life. Besides that, lazy people started leading the life of a recluse because they wanted to escape from their responsibilities and problems of life. The hermits and the recluses roaming around are spending their lives at places of pilgrimage, keeping away from society, where they get to eat for free or get some money in charity. They are happy, leading their lives doing nothing.

Demerits of a common worldly man

The scene is the same in the life of a worldly man. Having attained human birth, a person is born in the world and becomes a worldly man. Man has got completely entangled in this illusory material world. He has also ignorantly taught his children to lead their lives with false beliefs, blind rituals, and material values.

A Bright worldly man is free from all these demerits of a recluse and a worldly man. Adopting the best qualities of both the recluse and the worldly man, a Bright worldly person attains liberation in life while leading an active life.

Light the lamp of Truth.
With new understanding, enter the life of prosperity.
Consider money as a means
and learn the secret of strengthening it.

24

Contemplation

Let us summarize the rules of prosperity:

- Always bear in mind that money is a powerful means, but not the end in itself.
- Inculcate the habit of savings by making a budget.
- Divide your earnings into ten equal parts and cover all your expenses with nine parts, leaving one part for savings or careful investment.
- Be aware of all your expenses; you should know how your money is being spent.
- Whenever you go shopping, always remember to ask yourself whether whatever you are going to buy is your 'need' or 'want'.
- Along with savings, also learn to grow your money.

- Always remember that there is never a money problem; the only problem is dearth of ideas.
- Respect money and allow it to flow in your life at the right speed, without placing any blocks in its path.
- Focus on what you receive in exchange for money, rather than focusing on "Here goes my money!"
- Make a magic box for the desires that you cannot fulfill with the nine parts.
- Do not indulge in fraudulent quick-rich schemes (or scams!).
- One of the important laws related to money to be borne in mind is: 'You grow by what you give; you just survive by what you get.' Till date, you have progressed due to whatever you have given.
- When you give what belongs to you, it will come back to you multifold. Understanding this principle of nature, learn to give to yourself too.
- Be instrumental for others' wellbeing and progress and help them solve their problems. These are the seeds of faith that you can consciously sow. Never forget to sow these seeds.
- Sow the seeds of faith from your side and wait patiently for them to sprout; do not leave in a hurry.
- Do not shy away from hard work if you want to earn money. Instead awaken. People, who do not avoid hard work and do not consider any work to be inferior, are never out of occupation. They never get laid off.
- Those, who have interest in learning and keep an eye on people's knowledge, are the ones who know accounts in the right sense. They do not postpone depositing their funds in the bank due to laziness and do not spend carelessly. They know the formula:

    Money problems = Carelessness + Laziness + Wrong habits − Understanding

- By the power of your positive and creative thinking, create such things that are the present or future needs of people. By doing so, you will never face shortage of money.
- Donate Money without being stingy or obsessed about hoarding money.

These are the secrets of prosperity. Apply these secrets in your life and attain abundant wealth, not just money, but also health, love, time, attention, friendship, and spiritual growth.

Some Points for Contemplation

False beliefs

What are the false beliefs you had related to money, that were brought to light while reading this book?

_____

_____

_____

Savings Plan

After reading this book, what plan have you worked out for saving money? If you haven't made any plan as yet, then do reflect on it and write it down.

_____

_____

_____

Ability

After reading this book, what activities are you going to begin to enhance your skills and abilities?

_____

_____

_____

Blocks

What are the blocks you have placed in the flow of money in the past, or even now?

_____

_____

_____

Seed of faith

What seeds of faith are you going to sow in your life, and how?

(Money, friendship, time, service, encouraging words, giving advice, giving ideas, praying, listening to someone's sorrows, providing help, giving gifts, giving unconditional love, charity, etc.)

_____

_____

_____

• • •

You can send your opinion or feedback on this book to:
Tej Gyan Foundation, P.O. Box 25, Pimpri Colony,
Pimpri, Pune – 411017, Maharashtra, INDIA
Email: englishbooks@tejgyan.org

About Sirshree

Sirshree's spiritual quest, which began during his childhood, led him on a journey through various schools of thought and prevalent meditation practices. His overpowering desire to attain the Truth made him relinquish his teaching profession. After a long period of contemplation on the truth of life, his spiritual quest culminated in the attainment of the ultimate truth. Since then, over the last two decades, he has dedicated his life toward elevating mass consciousness and making spiritual pursuit simple and accessible to all.

Sirshree espouses, **"All paths that lead to the truth begin differently, but culminate at the same point – understanding. Understanding is complete in itself. Listening to this understanding is enough to attain the truth."**

Sirshree has delivered more than 3000 discourses that throw light on this understanding, simplify various aspects of life and unravel missing links in spirituality. He delivers the understanding in casual contemporary language by weaving profound aspects into analogies, parables and humor that provoke one to contemplate.

To make it possible for people from all walks of life to directly experience this understanding, Sirshree has designed the *Maha Aasmani Param Gyan Shivir* – a retreat designed as a comprehensive system for imparting wisdom. This system for wisdom, which has been accredited with ISO 9001:2015 certification, has inspired thousands of seekers from all walks of life to progress on their journey of the Truth. This system makes the wisdom accessible to every human being, regardless of religion, caste, social strata, country or belief system.

Sirshree is the founder of Tej Gyan Foundation, a no-profit organization committed to raising mass consciousness with branches in India, the United States, Europe and Asia-Pacific. Sirshree's retreats have transformed the lives of thousands and his teachings have inspired various social initiatives for raising global consciousness.

His published work includes more than 100 books, some of which have been translated in more than 10 languages and published by leading publishers. Sirshree's books provide profound and practical reading on existential subjects like emotional maturity, harmony in relationships, developing self-belief, overcoming stress and anxiety, and dealing with the question of life-beyond-death, to name a few. His literature on core spirituality expounds the deeper meaning of self-realization and self-stabilization, unravelling missing links in the understanding of karma, wisdom, devotion, meditation and consciousness.

Various luminaries and celebrities like His Holiness the Dalai Lama, publishers Mr. Reid Tracy, Ms. Tami Simon and Yoga Master Dr. B. K. S. Iyengar have released Sirshree's books and lauded his work. "The Source" book series, authored by Sirshree, has sold over 10 million copies in 5 years. His book, "The Warrior's Mirror", published by Penguin, was featured in the Limca Book of Records for being released on the same day in 11 languages.

Tejgyan... The Road Ahead

What is Tejgyan?

Tejgyan is the wisdom of the existential truth, which is beyond duality. "Gyan" is a term commonly used for "knowledge". Tejgyan is the wisdom beyond knowledge and ignorance. It is understanding that arises from direct experience of the final truth. It is what sets us free from the limitations of the mind and opens us to our highest potential.

In today's world, there are people who feel disharmony and are desperately trying to achieve balance in an unpredictable life. Tejgyan helps them in harmonizing with their true nature, the Self, thereby restoring balance in all aspects of their lives.

And then, there are those who are successful, but feel a sense of emptiness within. Tejgyan provides them fulfilment and helps them to embark on a journey towards self-realization. There are others who feel lost and are seeking the meaning of life. Tejgyan helps them to realize the true purpose of human life.

All this is possible with Tejgyan due to a very simple reason. The experience of the ultimate truth (God or Pure consciousness) is always available. The direct experience of this truth is possible provided the right method is known. Tejgyan is that method, that understanding.

The understanding of Tejgyan makes it possible to lead a life of freedom from fear, worry, anger and stress. It helps in attaining physical vitality, emotional strength and stability, harmony in relationships, financial freedom and spiritual progress.

At Tej Gyan Foundation, Sirshree imparts this understanding through a System for Wisdom – a series of retreats that guides participants step by step towards realizing the true Self, being established in the experience of self-realization, and expressing its qualities. This system for wisdom has been accredited with the ISO 9001:2015 certification.

Maha Aasmani Param Gyan Shivir

"**Maha Aasmani Param Gyan Shivir**" is the flagship Self-realization retreat offered by Tej Gyan Foundation. The retreat is conducted in Hindi. The teachings of the retreat are non-denominational (secular).

This residential retreat is held for 3 to 5 days at the foundation's MaNaN Ashram amidst the glory of the mountains and the pristine beauty of nature. The Ashram is located at the outskirts of the city of Pune in India, and is well connected by air, road and rail. The retreat is also held at other centres of Tej Gyan Foundation across the world.

You can participate in this retreat to attain ageless wisdom through a unique System for Wisdom so that you can:

1. Discover "Who am I" through direct experience.
2. Learn to abide in pure consciousness while functioning in the world, allowing the qualities of consciousness like peace, love, joy, compassion, abundance and creativity to manifest.
3. Acquire simple tools to use in everyday life, which help quiet the chattering mind.
4. Get practical techniques to be in the present and connect to the source of all answers within (the inner guru).
5. Discover missing links in the practices of Meditation (*Dhyana*), Action (*Karma*), Wisdom (*Gyana*) and Devotion (*Bhakti*).
6. Understand the nature of your body-mind mechanism to attain freedom form its tendencies.
7. Learn practical methods to shift from mind-centered living to consciousness-centered living.

A Mini-retreat is also conducted, especially for teenagers (14 to 16 years of age) during summer and winter vacations.

To register for retreats, visit www.tejgyan.org,
contact (+91) 9921008060, or email mail@tejgyan.com

About Tej Gyan Foundation

Tej Gyan Foundation (TGF) was established with the mission of creating a highly evolved society through all-round development of every individual that transforms all the facets of their lives. It is a non-profit organization, founded on the teachings of Sirshree.

The Foundation has received the ISO certification (ISO 9001:2015) for its system of imparting wisdom. It has centres all across India as well as in other countries. The motto of Tej Gyan Foundation is 'Happy Thoughts'.

At the core of the philosophy of Tejgyan is the Power of Acceptance. Acceptance has profound meaning and is at the core of our Being. It is Acceptance that brings forth true love, joy and peace.

Symbol of Acceptance

The Symbol of Acceptance – shown above – is a representation of this truth. The symbol represents brackets. Whatever occurs in life falls within these brackets that signify acceptance of whatever is. Hence, this symbol forms the centerpiece of the Foundation's MaNaN Ashram.

The Foundation is creating a highly evolved society through:
- Tejgyan Programs (Retreats, YouTube Webcasts)
- Tejgyan Books and Apps
- Tejgyan Projects (Value education, Women empowerment, Peace initiatives)

The Foundation undertakes projects to elevate the level of consciousness among students, youth, women, senior citizens, teachers, doctors, leaders, professionals, corporate and Government organizations, police force, prisoners etc.

Good News!

Maha Aasmani Param Gyan Retreat
is now conducted ONLINE in Hindi!

You can participate in the retreat from the convenience of your home. The retreat is conducted in 3 parts during weekends:

1. The Foundation Truth retreat

2. The Bright Responsibility retreat

3. The Maha Aasmani final retreat

For more details, please call: +91 9921008060, +91 9921008075

To register, visit: https://www.tejgyanglobal.org/mareg

Books can be delivered at your doorstep by registered post or courier. You can request the same through postal money order or pay by VPP. Please send the money order to either of the following two addresses:

WOW Publishings Pvt. Ltd.

1. Registered Office: E-4, Vaibhav Nagar, Near Tapovan Mandir, Pimpri, Pune - 411017.

2. Post Box No. 36, Pimpri Colony Post Office, Pimpri, Pune - 411017

Phone No: (+91) 9011013210 / 9623457873

You can also order your copy at the online store:

www.gethappythoughts.org

*Free Shipping plus 10% Discount on purchases above Rs. 500/-

SELECT BOOKS AUTHORED BY SIRSHREE

   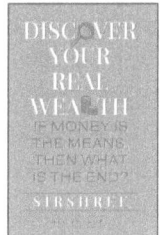

To order these and other books authored by Sirshree
Visit **www.gethappythoughts.org**

For further details contact:
Tejgyan Global Foundation
Registered Office:
Happy Thoughts Building, Vikrant Complex, Near Tapovan Mandir, Pimpri, Pune 411017, Maharashtra, India.
Contact No: 020-27411240, 27412576
Email: mail@tejgyan.com

MaNaN Ashram:
Survey No. 43, Sanas Nagar, Nandoshi gaon, Kirkatwadi Phata, Sinhagad Road, Tal. Haveli, Dist. Pune 411024, Maharashtra, India.
Contact No: 992100 8060.
Hyderabad: 9885558100, Bangalore: 9880412588,
Delhi : 9891059875, Nashik: 9326967980, Mumbai: 9373440985

For accessing our unique 'System for Wisdom' from self-help to self-realization, please follow us on:

	Website Online Shopping/ Blog	www.tejgyan.org www.gethappythoughts.org
	Video Channel	www.youtube.com/tejgyan For Q&A videos: http://goo.gl/YA81DQ
	Social networking	www.facebook.com/tejgyan
	Social networking	www.twitter.com/sirshree
	Internet Radio	http://www.tejgyan.org/internetradio.aspx

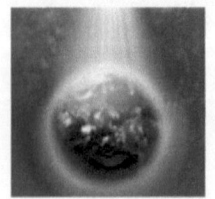

Pray for World Peace along with thousands of others every day at 09:09am and 09:09pm

Divine Light of Love, Bliss and Peace is Showering;
The Golden Light of Higher Consciousness is Rising;
All negativity on Earth is Dissolving;
Everyone is in Peace and Blissfully Shining;
O God, Gratitude for Everything!

www.ingramcontent.com/pod-product-compliance
Lightning Source LLC
LaVergne TN
LVHW041854070526
838199LV00045BB/1604